Burke

Past Masters

AQUINAS Anthony Kenny
BACON Anthony Quinton
BURKE C. B. Macpherson
DANTE George Holmes
GALILEO Stillman Drake

HOMER Jasper Griffin
HUME A. J. Ayer
JESUS Humphrey Carpenter
MARX Peter Singer
PASCAL Alban Krailsheimer

Forthcoming

ARISTOTLE Jonathan Barnes
AUGUSTINE Henry Chadwick
BACH Denis Arnold
BAYLE Elisabeth Labrousse
BERGSON Leszek Kolakowski
BERKELEY J. O. Urmson
JOSEPH BUTLER R. G. Frey
CARLYLE A. L. Le Quesne
COBBETT Raymond Williams
CONFUCIUS Raymond Dawson
COPERNICUS Owen
  Gingerich
DARWIN Jonathan Howard
DIDEROT Peter France
ENGELS Terrell Carver
ERASMUS James McConica
GIBBON John Burrow
GODWIN Alan Ryan
GOETHE J. P. Stern
HEGEL Peter Singer
HERZEN Aileen Kelly
JEFFERSON Jack P. Greene

LAMARCK L. J. Jordanova
LINNAEUS W. T. Stearn
LOCKE John Dunn
MACHIAVELLI Quentin
  Skinner
MALTHUS Gertrude
  Himmelfarb
MILL William Thomas
MONTAIGNE Peter Burke
THOMAS MORE Anthony
  Kenny
MORRIS Peter Stansky
NEWMAN Owen Chadwick
NEWTON P. M. Rattansi
PLATO R. M. Hare
ROUSSEAU John McManners
ST PAUL Tom Mills
SHAKESPEARE Germaine
  Greer
ADAM SMITH A. W. Coats
TOLSTOY Henry Gifford

and others

C. B. Macpherson

BURKE

Oxford Toronto Melbourne
OXFORD UNIVERSITY PRESS
1980

Oxford University Press, Walton Street, Oxford OX2 6DP

London Glasgow New York Toronto
Delhi Bombay Calcutta Madras Karachi
Kuala Lumpur Singapore Jakarta Hong Kong Tokyo
Nairobi Dar es Salaam Cape Town
Melbourne Wellington

and associate companies in
Beirut Berlin Ibadan Mexico City

First published as an Oxford University Press paperback
1980 and simultaneously in a hardback edition

British Library Cataloguing in Publication Data
Macpherson, Crawford Brough
Burke. – (Past masters).
1. Burke, Edmund, b. 1729
I. Series
320I.0I JC176 B83
ISBN 0–19–287519–1
ISBN 0–19–287518–3 Pbk

Printed in Great Britain by
Cox & Wyman Ltd, Reading

Contents

Abbreviations *vii*

1 The Burke problem *1*

2 The Irish adventurer *8*

3 The English politician *13*

4 The Anglo-European wasp *38*

5 The bourgeois political economist *51*

6 Burke for the late twentieth century? *71*

Note on sources *75*

Further reading *77*

Index *78*

Abbreviations

References in the text to Burke's writings are given by initial letters representing the title of the work, followed by a volume and page reference. Except for two references noted below (the *Correspondence* and the *Reflections*), the volume and page references are to the sixteen-volume *Works* published by Rivington, London 1815–27.

A	Appeal from the New to the Old Whigs
AE	Speech on the Army Estimates
AT	Speech on American Taxation
C	*The Correspondence of Edmund Burke* (ed. T. W. Copeland, Cambridge University Press, 1958–70)
CC	Speech on ... Conciliation with the Colonies
CI	Speech at the Close of the Impeachment
EB	Speech to the Electors of Bristol at the Conclusion of the Poll
EI	Speech on Fox's East-India Bill
ER	Speech on Economical Reform
HL	Letter to Sir Hercules Langrishe
LSB	Letter to the Sheriffs of Bristol on the Affairs of America
NA	Letter to a Member of the National Assembly
NL	Letter to a Noble Lord
O	Observations on ... the Present State of the Nation
OI	Speech on Opening the Articles of Impeachment
P	Tract on the Popery Laws
PD	Thoughts on the Cause of the Present Discontents

R   *Reflections on the Revolution in France* (ed. Conor Cruise O'Brien, Penguin, Harmondsworth, 1969)

RCP   Speech on the State of Representation of the Commons in Parliament

RP 1 First Letter on a Regicide Peace

RP 3 Third letter on a Regicide Peace

S   Thoughts and Details on Scarcity

SB   Philosophical Enquiry into the Origin of our Ideas of the Sublime and Beautiful

V   Vindication of Natural Society

1 The Burke problem

That there is a Burke problem is a testimony to the continuing interest there has been in his work in the two centuries since it was done. Burke lived from 1729 to 1797, was an English Member of Parliament from 1766 to 1794, and was an increasingly prominent writer and speaker, mainly on political issues, from 1756 to 1797. Why is he still celebrated? How can his treatment of issues important in the eighteenth century still evoke interest and admiration and criticism? The answers to these questions will become evident as this study proceeds.

Towards the end of his life Burke wrote dismissively, and with some satisfaction, of a once-renowned writer with whose principles he disagreed and whose work he had parodied in his own first published work thirty years earlier: 'Who now reads Bolingbroke? Who ever read him through? Ask the booksellers of London what is become of all these lights of the world.' (R 186. Burke was here bracketing with Bolingbroke several eighteenth-century deists and freethinkers.)

To assess the worth of a writer's works by their popularity or neglect, in his own time or later, is not the kind of judgement that commends itself nowadays to literary critics or philosophers or historians of ideas. But Burke was none of these. He was a devoted and principled politician, an acclaimed House of Commons orator, and a superb pamphleteer. In those capacities he did not scruple, in taunting those he opposed, to use any handy opprobrium.

We ought not to apply the same measures to Burke himself. If we were to do so, we should have to ask why, in spite of much present conservative lip-service to his name, none of the several nineteenth- and early twentieth-century editions of his works has been kept in print, and why only his most famous work, the *Reflections on the Revolution in France*, is now readily obtainable. But we should at the same time have to

notice that scholarly interest in Burke has been on the increase
for some decades now, and shows few signs of diminishing. A
Burke Newsletter was inaugurated in 1959 by some American
scholars intent on developing scholarly discussion of Burke;
this was broadened in 1967 to become *Studies in Burke and His
Time*; only in 1979 was Burke demoted from the title, when a
continuation of the journal, still further broadened, appeared
as *The Eighteenth Century: Theory and Interpretation.* A substantial study of Burke's career and his thought was published
in two volumes (1957 and 1964) by another American scholar.
A complete edition of Burke's correspondence, begun as soon as
the main collection of his private papers had been made available to scholars, resulted in a nine-volume edition of his *Correspondence* completed in 1970. The 1950s and 60s saw the
publication of four books devoted to Burke's thought and
placing him in the Natural Law tradition, which goes back
beyond the middle ages. More recently there has been a short
but excellent study of his political ideas which effectively
reduces some of the claims that had been made for him. And
most recently – the ultimate accolade nowadays – he has been
made the subject of a thoroughgoing psychohistorical study.

When all this is taken into account, Burke comes out not too
badly on a market computation. But any such computation
would not only be superficial, it would take us away from the
intriguing questions. Why has his reputation, over the last two
hundred years, been based on such varying interpretations of
his work? Can they all have some validity? And, in so far as
there is an underlying consistency in all of his thought, what is
its basis?

There is no dispute about the wide variations in the way he
has been seen, and the grounds on which his writings have been
celebrated. Through most of his active life his work had been
valued by moderate reforming Whigs as a reasoned support of
their position, as in his exposure of the inroads he saw being
made on the independence of Parliament by the Court, his case
against the government's policy on the American colonies, and
his sustained attack on the arbitrary rule of the chartered East

India Company. Then quite suddenly, in the last decade of his life, he appeared in a new character, as the scourge of the liberal egalitarian ideas unleashed by the French Revolution, the great defender of traditional hierarchical society against the menacing theory and practice of that revolution. This brought him a much wider acclaim than any he had previously enjoyed, and from a different quarter. George III, of whose policies Burke had been a very vocal critic, went so far as to say, after the publication of Burke's *Reflections on the Revolution in France* (1790), 'You have been of use to us all ... I know that there is no Man who calls himself a Gentleman who must not think himself obliged to you, for you have supported the cause of the Gentlemen (c 6.239). Other crowned heads in Europe were equally impressed. Even the rationalist Edward Gibbon, who could not have relished Burke's insistence that the Christian religion was the indispensable basis of political stability, congratulated Burke on his *Reflections* as 'a most admirable medicine against the French disease'. The impression of Burke as the arch-conservative seemed indelibly fixed: his crusade against the French Revolution had eclipsed all his other works.

But in the nineteenth century Burke was made over into a utilitarian liberal. His French crusade was set aside as something of an aberration. Attention was focused instead on his earlier writings and speeches. The record there was very different: vigorous foe of the Court party, of autocratic government, of the kinds of British imperialism then prevailing in America and Ireland and India; friend of the commercial interest, informed critic of economic policies, and advocate of a self-regulating market economy; friend of religious toleration; and of course defender of the Whig Revolution. Here then was a worthy successor to John Locke, the founding father of the Whig theory, whose work was now a century out of date. In that character he was held in contempt by Marx, who called him 'the celebrated sophist and sycophant' and 'an out and out vulgar bourgeois'; but the nineteenth-century liberals honoured him for that position. John Morley, leading liberal spokesman of the late nineteenth century, set his seal on the liberal version of Burke in two books, in which Burke was portrayed as a liberal constitutionalist whose later illiberal counter-revolutionary writings were to be treated with reserve and on which judgement was to be held in abeyance. The historian Henry Thomas Buckle was more forthright, holding that in his French period Burke had gone out of his mind, that 'the balance tottered', and 'the proportions of that gigantic intellect were disturbed'.

The liberal Burke lasted well into the twentieth century. Even Harold Laski, writing from a little outside the liberal tradition, could in 1920 applaud Burke as a liberal utilitarian, while noticing and deploring Burke's darker undemocratic side.

But the usual liberal portrait was unsatisfactory. It left too much out. It had no room for the equally authentic Burke who was a devoted defender of hierarchy, prescription and inherited rights, of custom and prejudice rather than abstract or mechanical reason, and who saw society as an organism embodying a divinely-given moral order. It was this Burke who was brought into fashion in the mid-twentieth century.

A reasonable case could be made for this view, and it was strongly urged by those who made Burke over into a Natural Law man. Coincidentally, the new portrait filled a new need in the 1950s: in reviving Burke the crusader against radicalism, it discovered a welcome ideological support for the cold war crusade against the apprehended threat of Soviet communism.

But the Natural Law version of Burke is just as unsatisfactory as was the liberal utilitarian version. Both are incomplete. Both fail to resolve, indeed largely fail to see, the seeming incoherence between Burke the traditionalist and Burke the bourgeois liberal. How could the same man be at once the defender of a hierarchical order and the proponent of a liberal market society? There is no way out by postulating a change in his views over time, for, as we shall see, both positions were asserted most explicitly in the same works of the 1790s. Nowhere in the two-hundred-year see-saw of images of Burke is this problem adequately faced.

I shall suggest, in Chapter 5, that the key to this problem lies in Burke's quality as a political economist. There is no doubt that in everything he wrote and did, he venerated the traditional order. But his traditional order was already a capitalist order. He saw that it was so, and wished it to be more freely so. He had no romantic yearning for a bygone feudal order and no respect for such remnants of it as still survived, notably in the royal household, as is evident from his caustic remarks in the *Speech on Economical Reform* (1780). He lived in the present, and made it his business to study the economic consequences of actual and projected state policies. As M.P. for Bristol (1775-80) he could scarcely have done otherwise, for Bristol was then one of the greatest commercial ports in England. But his interest in economic affairs had, as we shall see in some detail, begun earlier and lasted longer than his connection with Bristol. He could, as he did, claim not unreasonably to be as well, or better, versed in political economy than any other politician of his time. When in one of his flights of rhetoric he inveighed against the age of 'sophisters, oeconomists, and calculators' (R 170) he allowed himself to forget his own quite valid claims as a political economist. Indeed, his most explicit statement of his economic assumptions came first in that full-dress defence of the old order, the *Reflections* (1790), and then more fully in the *Thoughts and Details on Scarcity* (1795) and the *Letters on a Regicide Peace* (1796-7). There is thus a prima facie case for seeking in Burke's political economy a resolution of this central problem of coherence.

A secondary problem of consistency may be seen in his ambivalence about the English aristocracy. How, we may ask, could he, the staunch supporter of inheritance and prescription as the true basis of property rights and social stability, have composed and published his *Letter to a Noble Lord* (1796), a vitriolic attack on the Duke of Bedford, a great aristocrat, who basked in an enormous inherited wealth to which prescriptive right gave him a clear title? How uphold, as a matter of principle, present property, however it may have originated in old violence, and excoriate the Duke whose property, as Burke was at pains to point out, had originated in Henry VIII's confiscations from some of the ancient nobility and his pillage of the Church? This is a very minor problem of consistency, nothing like as important as the central one. It is only worth separate notice because it comes from the circumstances of Burke's personal career and is not entirely resolved by the resolution of the central problem. His ambivalence about the aristocracy was not a matter of the apparent but unreal inconsistency between his traditionalist and his bourgeois liberal positions; it was not Burke the bourgeois, but Burke the ranker, never fully accepted by those to whom he had attached himself, who composed the *Letter to a Noble Lord*.

A clue is to be found in the fact that Burke, in his whole career as an English politician and propagandist, was a parvenu, and moreover an Irish parvenu. He was, and was seen by opponents to be, an Irish adventurer intent on making his mark in English politics. He made a mark, but one not as distinguished as he might well have thought his talents and energy had entitled him to. As the protégé and very effective workhorse of one of the great Whig connections – the party of the Rockingham Whigs, which was in office twice, though briefly each time, during Burke's adherence – he climbed part of the way up the political ladder but never got near the top. He was never admitted to cabinet rank, to which his energy, his ability and his party service might well be thought to have entitled him. All he got was an honorific appointment as a privy councillor, which entitled him to the prefix The Right Honourable, and, from 1782 to 1784, the post of Paymaster General. Although he privately disclaimed any expectation of a cabinet position – he must have realised that he lacked the usual qualfications of great wealth or noble title – it may not be too much to see in this a source of his ambivalence about the aristocracy. The brief review, in the following chapter, of the circumstances of his entry into and career within English political society may lend some support to this view.

A third seeming inconsistency, with which Burke was sometimes reproached by his critics, can be dismissed very quickly: that is, the alleged discrepancy between his positions on the

American and the French Revolutions. No one who reads Burke at all attentively could find any contradiction between his defence of the American Revolution (when that revolution had been made inevitable by the policies of the English government, of which Burke had been a vigorous opponent), and his implacable opposition, a decade later, to the French Revolution. Both positions were firmly grounded in his attachment to the principles he found in the English Whig Revolution of 1689, principles which in his view justified the American colonists in 1776 but utterly ruled out the pretensions of the French revolutionaries and their English adherents after 1789. There is no inconsistency here, and no change of ground.

Thus the central Burke problem which is still of considerable interest in our own time is the question of the coherence of his two seemingly opposite positions: the defender of a hierarchical establishment, and the market liberal. This question, I suggest, transcends the debate, which claimed most attention a few decades ago, as to whether he was a utilitarian or a Natural Law man. It raises more acutely the relevance of Burke's work to one of the main political debates in Western societies in the late twentieth century. And it suggests a final question for our consideration: how far, if at all, can Burke properly be enlisted by conservatives or liberals today?

2 The Irish adventurer

Edmund Burke was born in Dublin in January 1729, the second son of a Protestant father and a Roman Catholic mother. The family was well-to-do, the father being a successful practising lawyer in Dublin. Burke grew up in Dublin, except for a few years which he spent as a young boy in the country with his mother's family in the south of Ireland for reasons of his health. He had an excellent education, first at a Quaker boarding school and then at Trinity College, Dublin. It was a strong classical education, the effects of which were evident throughout his life. Modernists may doubt whether Burke's superb command of the English language was due at all to his training in the classical languages, but no one can doubt that those languages stayed with him: his speeches, pamphlets and books are studded with Latin tags (and a few Greek) and with quotations from classical authors used quite unselfconsciously. His use of these is revealing in another way. He almost never gave an English translation, even though sometimes the completion of an argument he was making depended on his hearers or readers understanding a Latin quotation. It is clear that Burke was speaking and writing for educated gentlemen only: his prose is a far cry from Tom Paine's. This tells us something also about the composition of the eighteenth-century House of Commons, to whose members a very large part of Burke's advocacy was addressed.

Burke's ambivalence about the aristocracy may be said to have begun in his student days at Trinity College, Dublin. He saw, and resented, the worse than colonial status to which the bulk of the population of Ireland was reduced by the heavily aristocratic establishment. He was deeply angered by the brutal poverty in which the peasantry were, as he saw it, kept by the decadent aristocratic rich, who made no effort to manage their estates efficiently and did nothing to encourage – who indeed actively discouraged – their tenants becoming industrious yeomen. His remarkable outbursts on this were published in a weekly paper, *The Reformer*, which Burke and some friends at Trinity produced for three months in the winter and spring of 1748, and most of which Burke himself wrote. This was no mere undergraduate paper: modelled on the *Spectator*, it was addressed to the educated Dublin public, and had very satisfactory sales.

But while Burke was merciless at that time towards the idle rich he was by no means a leveller. As Kramnick has pointed out, Burke's position then was substantially a bourgeois one: property should be secure, but the duty of proprietors was to improve their properties so as to increase the wealth of the nation to the benefit of all classes. It would not be too much to see in this undergraduate performance the manifesto of a thrusting young man who was aware that he had unusual talent but realised that his future could only be that of a self-made man. This would require coming to terms with the establishment, and moving within it. But that prospect was not too daunting, since he already subscribed to its cardinal value, the sanctity of property. His task would be to persuade his betters that they would be still better if they would anchor their property in something other than absentee landlordism. Had he confined his efforts to Ireland this would have been difficult. But in England, where many of the great aristocratic landowners were already operating on improving commercial principles, this was not such a problem. This would give Burke the opening he needed, and not long afterwards he was able to take advantage of it.

An Irishman Burke remained. But, through his father's desire that Edmund should follow in his footsteps by making a career in the law, his horizon broadened beyond Ireland. For to fit him for that career, he had to be sent to London to become qualified in English law. Burke moved to London in the spring of 1750, aged twenty-one, as a law student enrolled in Middle Temple. He applied himself assiduously enough at first to jurisprudence, but his heart was rather in literature and his am-

bition became a career in literature. In later years he spoke
highly of the discipline of jurisprudence, but he had no taste
for a life as a practising lawyer. Law studies dropped into the
background, displaced by literary avocations.

Six years later, the first fruit of his literary ambition was
realised: a leading London publisher brought out a book by him
which won immediate and favourable notice, *A Vindication of
Natural Society* (first edition 1756, second edition 1757). It
was, perhaps surprisingly in view of Burke's later contempt for
abstract philosophising, an essay in abstract social philosophy.
But there is no contradiction here, for it was an attack on the
application of abstract theory, especially Rousseau's, to politics.
A satirical work, it set out to show that the then modish case
that Bolingbroke had made for *natural* as opposed to *acquired*
religion could be paralleled by a case for *natural* as opposed to
civil society and government. Burke's point was that simplistic
claims for the natural would entail the destruction of all civil
society and government. The *Vindication* was published
anonymously, and it was so well done that it was thought by
some to be by Bolingbroke himself. The next year a second
edition appeared with a preface explaining its satirical intent.

At the same time Burke produced a short treatise on aesthetics, *A Philosophical Enquiry into the Origin of our Ideas of
the Sublime and Beautiful* (first edition 1757, second edition
1759), which brought him still more to the attention of literary
London. These two books, a remarkable achievement for a
young man of twenty-seven, brought him rapidly into the best
literary and artistic circles in London. He was taken up, and
held his own as a welcome conversationalist, by Goldsmith,
Reynolds, Garrick, Johnson and Sheridan, and five years later
was a charter member of 'the Club', which numbered these as
well as other worthies such as Adam Smith.

However, by 1757 he was forced to the conclusion that his
niche in literary London gave too uncertain a prospect of a
stable income. The importance of a steady income became a
pressing matter when he married in March 1757. Intending to
start a family very soon (which he did), he took a serious view

of the obligations of a gentleman. He tried his hand next at history. There was a good market for historical works: Hume, for instance, had been working for some time on his large-scale *History*, of which the first two volumes came out in 1754 and 1757. Dodsley, who had published Burke's first two books, contracted with him for a one-volume history of England. Burke produced a fair amount of this, but, starting from the earliest conjectural times he brought it only to the year 1216 before giving it up. It was not published in Burke's own lifetime: what he had done was published posthumously as *An Essay Towards an Abridgement of the English History*.

Then, in April 1758, by which time his family obligations had been increased by the birth of his first son, he moved on to Grub Street, albeit a rather superior station in that street. His subsequent description of himself as a Grub Street scribbler (RP3 8.366) was rather disingenuous, for his contract with Dodsley was to compile, and indeed write most of, an annual 500-page review of history, politics and literature, for an annual payment of £100, a substantial sum in those days. The first issue of the *Annual Register*, for 1758, was completed by May 1759, and Burke continued to run it until about 1776, when he appears to have relinquished the editorship, although still writing book reviews and making himself available for general advice.

But this was still not enough for Burke's ambition. In 1759 he began the apprenticeship to English politics which was to lead him into his illustrious English and European career. It began with his being taken up by an M.P. and office-holder, William Gerard Hamilton, who in 1761 became chief secretary to the Lord Lieutenant of Ireland and asked Burke to go with him as private secretary. That lasted for four years. It brought Burke into Irish affairs, which he now had to see from the viewpoint of the English managers. He broke with Hamilton in 1765, rather acrimoniously, on personal rather than political grounds (C 1.178–86). Having been out of circulation in the literary world for six years, he was left with neither political nor literary career prospects.

His future seemed gloomy, but his merits were not unknown.

In July 1765 he was taken on as private secretary to the Marquis of Rockingham, the great Whig peer who was just then to become Prime Minister. Rockingham's first administration lasted only a year, but he had a high enough estimate of Burke's worth that he kept him on as, in effect, the secretary of the Rockingham Whig party.

The Irish adventurer, the London littérateur, the Grub Street journalist, had entered the mainstream of English political life. He was easily found a seat in the House of Commons, in 1766, before he could have won one on his own reputation, so accommodating was the system of rotten boroughs, where a single peer, in this case Lord Verney, controlled the elections (in Wendover). Burke was kept in that seat until 1775 when he won a seat for Bristol on his own merits. And another seat was easily found for him after he had, in 1780, lost the Bristol seat by refusing to act as an instructed delegate of his constituents.

Burke was an M.P. continuously from 1766 to 1794. And it is on his actions as an M.P., his speeches in the House of Commons, and the pamphlets and more substantial works he published to vindicate his actions there, that his reputation rested for all but the last few years of his life. Then, his fame as the great crusader against the French Revolution and its English supporters drew attention away from everything else. But the work of his middle years was again given first place in the nineteenth-century liberal portrait of him. And the twentieth-century conservative reconstruction of Burke, while taking off from his last counter-revolutionary years, was far from rejecting his earlier thought. His conservative portraitists may have been over-eager to read back into his earlier thought the principles of his last crusade, but though they may not have seen the full measure of the continuity, they did see that there was a continuity in his steady veneration of the English Constitution (more accurately, of the principles he read into it). The work of his middle years is in any case an indispensable part of his thought, and to it we must now turn.

3 The English politician

Burke prided himself on being a hard-working practical politician, intent, in and out of the House of Commons, on exposing whatever abuses he found in the British system of government, and pressing for moderate reforms which would prevent future abuses whether at home or in the handling of the colonial empire in Ireland, America and India. His record of activity in this role is indeed impressive. But had he been no more than such an active politician his work would not now be of interest to any except eighteenth-century historians. What more was there? Why should his speeches and writings, most of which were partisan pleadings on some issue of the day, still command attention?

The liberal view in the nineteenth and twentieth centuries has been that they rightly command our attention because Burke infused every particular issue with general principles. He is credited with raising politics far above the mean and unprincipled skirmishing for office and spoils which it had become in the mid-eighteenth century with the disappearance of the old difference of principle between Whigs and Tories. He insisted that every issue should be debated in terms of some standard of justice or right or long-run human benefit, rather than of mere legal rights or short-run expediency; and this insistence, in the House of Commons and in pamphlets and books and speeches outside the House, compelled his opponents to move to that higher ground. Nineteenth- and twentieth-century liberals, who were apt to think that the liberalism of their own time needed the same sort of moral injection, could not but regard this as a significant achievement. Thus John Morley in 1867: 'he brought the dead Whig principles up from out of the grave, and kindled a life in them, which has only just flickered out forever in our own days'. And again:

. . . no one that ever lived used the general ideas of the thinker more successfully to judge the particular problems of the statesman. No one has ever come so close to the details of practical politics, and at the same time remembered that these can only be understood and only dealt with by the aid of the broad conceptions of political philosophy.

Similarly Harold Laski in 1920:

No English statesman has ever more firmly moved amid a mass of details to the principle they involve . . . He had an unerring eye for the eternal principles of politics. He knew that ideals must be harnessed to an Act of Parliament if they are not to cease their influence. Admitting while he did that politics must rest upon expediency, he never failed to find good reason why expediency should be identified with what he saw as right.

This liberal view of Burke, though couched in such extravagant terms, does not claim him as a great theorist or political philosopher: the only claim is that he revivified political practice by bringing it back to some moral principles. The liberals did not inquire how thorough or consistent those principles were.

They could not have claimed Burke as a theorist, for very good reason. During the whole period in which Burke could be claimed as a liberal, that is, down to 1790, Burke neither was nor wished to be a political theorist, and even after 1790 it was only against his will that he was forced into theorising. Scorn for abstract theory was a constant refrain of his output as a reforming politician. Again and again he argued that it was unrealistic, even disastrous, to try to deduce practical policy from abstract principles. Take for instance his position in the *Letter to the Sheriffs of Bristol on the Affairs of America* (1777): the few pages there on the great general question of liberty versus authority begin in scorn for, and lead on to a repudiation of, any such deductive reasoning:

It is melancholy as well as ridiculous, to observe the kind of reasoning with which the publick has been amused, in order to divert our minds from the common sense of our American policy. There are

people who have split and anatomised the doctrine of free government, as if it were an abstract question concerning metaphysical
liberty and necessity; and not a matter of moral prudence and natural feeling. They have disputed, whether liberty be a positive or a
negative idea; whether it does not consist in being governed by laws;
without considering what are the laws, or who are the makers;
whether man has any rights by nature; and whether all the property
he enjoys, be not the alms of his government, and his life itself their
favour and indulgence. . . . of another kind, speculations are let loose
as destructive to all authority, as the former are to all freedom; and
every government is called tyranny and usurpation which is not
formed on their fancies . . .
Civil freedom, gentlemen, is not, as many have endeavoured to
persuade you, a thing that lies hid in the depth of abstruse science. It
is a blessing and a benefit, not an abstract speculation; and all the
just reasoning that can be upon it, is of so coarse a texture, as
perfectly to suit the ordinary capacities of those who are to enjoy,
and of those who are to defend it. Far from any resemblance to those
propositions in geometry and metaphysicks, which admit no medium,
but must be true or false in all their latitude; social and civil freedom,
like all the other things in common life, are variously mixed and
modified, enjoyed in very different degrees, and shaped into an
infinite diversity of forms, according to the temper and circumstances of every community. (LSB 3. 183–5)

This particular rejection of abstract theory may well be ascribed to Burke's perception that its use by both sides in the war
of American Independence had contributed to their intransigence and was impeding a rational peace:

. . . whether liberty be advantageous or not, (for I know it is a
fashion to decry the very principle) none will dispute that peace is a
blessing; and peace must in the course of human affairs be frequently bought by some indulgence and toleration at least to liberty.
(ibid. 186)

Burke's appeal to the leaders of public opinion on both sides to
abandon their stand on theory was the only way he could
see to break out of the political impasse. Had he been a theorist,
his appropriate response would have been to expose the fallacies

of one or both of the two theoretical cases by a more adequate theoretical analysis; but that was not his way.

Similarly, in his efforts to restore the 'true' principles of the Whig settlement of 1689, he was practitioner, not theorist. A theorist would have seen a need to reconstruct Locke's theoretical justification of the principles of 1689, to rework it so as to meet the damaging criticisms implicit in the work of Hume (*Treatise of Human Nature*, 1739 and *Essays*, 1741–58), of Adam Ferguson (*Essay on the History of Civil Society*, 1767) and of John Millar (*The Origin of the Distinction of Ranks*, 1771), but again that was not Burke's way. The liberal view of Burke as a non-theorist seems amply vindicated.

The twentieth-century neo-conservative readings of Burke, on the contrary, rank him as a masterly political philosopher. Thus Parkin:

. . . while Burke's thought is by design a response to immediate contingencies, it is in no sense an uncontrolled or arbitrary response, but always, in his own eyes, under the guidance of moral principles, which . . . represent themselves unchanging truths of human life and community. . . . Burke's political thought . . . always leans toward a still centre of the most general and absolute belief. His ideas carry all the marks and associations of their origin, but they converge on a core of moral certainty freed finally from the relative and the contingent.

Similarly Stanlis, arguing that Burke's great achievement was to restore the classical and scholastic Natural Law to its rightful place as the fundamental moral principle of politics, holds that 'the true nature of Burke's cardinal political principles cannot be understood apart from its connection with the Natural Law', and that his political philosophy 'supplies a superb solution to the persistent confusions and doubts' of those who still rely on the utilitarian or positivist or materialist traditions. Stanlis goes on to assert:

In every important political problem he ever faced, in Irish, American, constitutional, economic, Indian, and French affairs, Burke *always* appealed to the Natural Law. What is more, by Natural Law

Burke always meant essentially the same thing, and he applied it as the ultimate test of justice and liberty in all human affairs.

These claims will be examined below, where I shall suggest that they are partly valid but wholly vacuous. But it is clear that for the neo-conservatives Burke was essentially a political philosopher.

In view of this disparity between the liberal and conservative views of Burke's stature as a thinker it seems worthwhile to examine, with more care than has been usual, just how much appeal to principle there is in his work.

It is common ground among all students of Burke's work that such appeal to principle as he did make was, throughout his political career, only what he thought would be efficacious in making his case on some current issue: British government policy in Ireland, America, India; the supposed assault of the Crown (and even, as in the Wilkes case, of Parliament) on British liberties; and finally, the menace of French Revolution principles, especially of their insidious influence in England, as in the propaganda of Priestley, Price, Paine, and their adherents.

The question that must now be asked is whether the clarity and depth of Burke's invocations of principle entitle him to the regard in which he has been held as a political thinker. We may begin by looking at his earliest published work, even though that was not yet linked to current issues, and go on to his mature years, in which all his thought was so linked. In this chapter we shall look at his work down to about 1790, reserving for the next two chapters a consideration of his work in the final decade of his life.

Burke's first two published works, the *Vindication of Natural Society* (1756) and the *Philosophical Enquiry into the Origin of our Ideas of the Sublime and Beautiful* (1757), were entirely theoretical. Although they were the product of Burke the dilettante intent on a literary career, and although Burke's admirers find little to praise in them, the *Vindication* at least is worth some attention. It was, as has been mentioned, an ironical supplement to Bolingbroke's case for natural as opposed to acquired religion. Pretending to extol natural (i.e. primitive) society, as Bolingbroke had extolled natural religion, Burke gives, as his subtitle puts it, 'a view of the miseries and evils arising to mankind from every species of artificial society', and this in terms as lurid as any in Rousseau's first two discourses. He concluded a long recital of the inequality, class oppression, and injustice evident in every civilised country, with a rhetorical question:

... if political society, in whatever form, has still made the many the property of the few; if it has introduced labours unnecessary, vices and diseases unknown, and pleasures incompatible with nature; if in all countries it abridges the lives of millions, and renders those of millions more utterly abject and miserable, shall we still worship so destructive an idol, and daily sacrifice to it our health, our liberty, and our peace? (v 1.76)

Only in the preface to the second edition did Burke make it clear that his whole argument was intended ironically. He meant the opposite of what he said. He wanted to demonstrate what an absurd conclusion (i.e. that we should abandon political society and return to a state of nature) could be reached by starting from such abstractions as 'natural' and 'artificial' society.

Two things about the *Vindication* are interesting in view of Burke's later work. First, he shows himself fully aware of the case that can be made against the political, legal, economic and moral order of eighteenth-century advanced societies. He sees constitutional monarchy, or mixed government, as a matter of cabals indifferent to oppression and injustice; his view of the British legal system is more scathing than Bentham's; his picture of the condition of the workers in mines and metal refineries is heart-rending; his recognition that in societies divided into rich and poor it is a constant and invariable law 'that those who labour most, enjoy the fewest things; and that those who labour not at all, have the greatest number of enjoyments' (v 1.70) foreshadows J. S. Mill's realistic perception of the same fact; his characterisation of the moral degeneracy of the rich echoes Rousseau's, and foreshadows Marx's, inclusion of the capitalists in the ranks of the alienated. It is clear that Burke was quite well aware, before he turned to a political career, how much the prevailing order had to answer for.

The second thing of interest is that in building his case, albeit satirical, against the theorists of political society, he proceeds by amassing concrete observable facts against abstract formulations. He declares that attention to real conditions must override a priori reasoning, and that actual conditions must be judged by moral standards. Already, then, Burke is firmly committed to the position which was to characterise his thinking as a practising politician. He was not led to that position by the exigencies of his political life. No change of outlook was required. Rather, that outlook, at once pragmatic and moral, made his choice of a political career a congenial one.

The theory of aesthetics presented in the *Sublime and Beautiful* is one of little theoretical interest. It has no moral dimension, apart from some homilies about the designs of the Creator, but proceeds inductively from simple physiological and psychological observations. It may be said to testify to Burke's empirical cast of mind, but it does not harness the empirical to the moral.

The first of Burke's writings on a specific political subject is the fragmentary *Tract on the Popery Laws*, which was drafted probably in 1761. He left it unfinished and unpublished, for evident reasons. He could not have published it at the time, for as private secretary to Hamilton, the chief secretary of the Lord Lieutenant of Ireland, Burke was then in effect a civil servant; and as soon as that constraint ended he was fully taken up with the exigencies of his immediately following connection with Lord Rockingham, which bent his energies to English political issues, as spokesman and ideas man for the Rockingham Whigs. Nevertheless, the *Tract* is worth our notice, for it displays already, at that early date, characteristics of Burke's thought which stayed with him throughout his life: the strenuous appeal to loosely-defined moral principles; the insistence that the application of general principles must be mediated by attention to the always complex current circumstances, and to the frailties of human nature; the use of empirical generalisations, drawn from observation and from history, to support his case against a priori reasoning from abstract principles; and his bourgeois assumptions about human nature.

The *Tract* is a sharp attack on the penal laws which had been enacted against the Irish Roman Catholics; laws which denied them many of the ordinary rights of citizenship and especially the full right to acquire and bequeath property in lands and goods. Those laws, Burke argued, were invalid because they contradicted the rationale of all law. He dismissed contemptuously Hobbes's doctrine that law is valid simply as the command of the sovereign. He asserted instead:

In reality there are two, and only two, foundations of Law; and they are both of them conditions, without which nothing can give it any force; I mean equity and utility. With respect to the former, it grows out of the great rule of equality, which is grounded upon our common nature, and which Philo, with propriety and beauty, calls the Mother of Justice. All human Laws are, properly speaking, only declaratory; they may alter the mode and application, but have no power over the substance of original justice. The other foundation of Law, which is utility, must be understood, not of partial or limited, but of general and publick utility, connected in the same manner with, and derived directly from, our rational nature; for any other utility may be the utility of a robber, but cannot be that of a citizen; the interest of the domestick enemy, and not that of a member of the Commonwealth. (P 9.351)

This sweeping appeal to the principles of equity and utility is reinforced by an invocation of natural rights:

Every body is satisfied that a conservation and secure enjoyment of our natural rights is the great and ultimate purpose of civil society; and that therefore all forms whatsoever of Government are only good as they are subservient to that purpose, to which they are entirely subordinate. (ibid. 364)

The argument then moves to a different kind of principle –

empirical generalisations. These are at two levels. First there is a sweeping generalisation about the necessary relation between economic prosperity (which is the substance of Burke's 'general and publick utility') and industriousness and property:

Those civil Constitutions, which promote industry, are such as facilitate the acquisition, secure the holding; enable the fixing, and suffer the alienation, of property. Every Law, which obstructs it in any part of this distribution, is, in proportion to the force and extent of the obstruction, a discouragement to industry. For a Law against property is a Law against industry, the latter having always the former, and nothing else, for its object. (ibid. 386)

The necessary connection between property and industry was in turn grounded on a generalisation about human motivation:

The desire of acquisition is always a passion of long views. Confine a man to momentary possession, and you at once cut off that laudable avarice, which every wise State has cherished as one of the first principles of its greatness. (ibid. 387)

The bourgeois individualist position that avarice is laudable, and that private acquisition ought to be promoted by the state on the utilitarian ground that acquisitiveness is the source of the wealth of nations – Burke's 'publick utility' – was more fully developed in Burke's writings in the 1790s, as will be noticed in Chapter 5. But already, thirty years earlier, Burke's position is evident. The more developed position, apparent in the *Reflections on the Revolution in France* (1790), set out most fully in *The Thoughts and Details on Scarcity* (1795), and reaffirmed in the *Letters on the Regicide Peace* (1796–7), was no new development in his thinking. It cannot be attributed to the extensive study of economic affairs he made in the 60s and 70s as party critic of government policies and advocate of 'economical reform' (1780): he came to that study with his fundamental bourgeois assumptions already settled. It is not surprising that Adam Smith, with whom he had probably not conversed until 1775, when Smith was elected to 'the Club', is reported to have said of Burke 'that he was the only man who, without communication, thought on these topics exactly as he did'. Burke's bourgeois predilection, unmentioned by many commentators and given little weight by others, was evidently firmly in place before the beginning of his career as a politician.

Burke's first substantial publication as an active politician, *Observations on a Late Publication Intituled the Present State of the Nation* (1769), was a defence of the brief Rockingham administration of 1765–6, by way of a slashing attack on a hostile pamphlet. Burke crushed the unfortunate author of that work under two hundred pages mainly of detailed economic analysis, but in the course of his argument he touched on one or two more general matters. There is a comment on the extent of the franchise, which he thought would be better decreased than increased, by the exclusion of 'the lower sort of voters' (o 2.136). There is a passing reference to the value of party, 'of having the great strong holds of government in well-united hands', allowing, however, sufficient room for 'healing coalitions' (ibid. 196). There is a presumption against any change in the Constitution: 'when you open it to enquiry in one part, where the enquiry will stop?' (ibid. 136). There is little invocation of principle, except for the denigration, which was so often repeated in his later work, of reasoning from abstract principles to constitutional change. He deplored 'agitating those vexatious questions [of the relation between sovereign power and individual freedom], which in truth rather belong to metaphysicks than politicks, and which can never be moved without shaking the foundations of the best governments that have ever been constituted by human wisdom' (ibid. 154). He urged that 'politicks ought to be adjusted, not to human reasonings, but to human nature; of which the reason is but a part, and by no means the greatest part' (ibid. 170).

His characteristic stance, making a principle of not deducing policy from principle, is already evident at the very beginning of his political career, not surprisingly, since, as we have seen, he brought that stance with him when he embarked on that career.

The *Thoughts on the Cause of the Present Discontents*

(1770), Burke's second substantial political pamphlet, is a spirited attack on what he saw as a surreptitious, and so far successful, attempt by the Court cabal to reduce Parliament to impotence. The essential and traditional role of the House of Commons, to check the Crown and the administration by refusing to vote the funds they wanted, had, he argued, been undermined by a subtle take-over. The Court cabal had managed to persuade Parliament to vote extraordinary additions to the Crown's revenue; additions which were not needed to uphold the dignity of the monarch, but were only needed, and were applied, to buy the support of the House for malign Court policies.

It was to stop this rot that Burke pressed the idea of party. Only if every administration's tenure was made to depend on the support of a declared party could this insidious undermining of the traditional function of Parliament be averted. If that principle were established, the tactics of the Court cabal could be defeated. Honest men, publicly committed to stand or fall together, could not be picked off, one by one, by offers of place or office:

Party is a body of men united, for promoting by their joint endeavours the national interest, upon some particular principle in which they are all agreed. (PD 2.335)

Burke's plea may be seen as no more than a manifesto for the Rockingham Whigs, who were the only group which then approximated to his criterion of party, in as much as their leaders were reluctant to take office except as a party. Or it may be seen as a pathbreaking work setting out the rationale of the party system and cabinet responsibility, which were to become in the nineteenth century essential features of the British system of government. But the claim that Burke thus charted and assisted the wave of the future can scarcely be sustained. He was proposing no more than a way out of the decay he saw around him: it was a short-run expedient for the immediate situation. He closed his plea for a party of honest men with a caution:

It is not every conjuncture which calls with equal force upon the activity of honest men; but critical exigencies now and then arise; and I am mistaken, if this be not one of them. (ibid. 341)

This is scarcely a foreshadowing of a regular two-party system of government.

Nor is there any appeal to moral principle. It is a plea to politicians to unite on the basis of shared principles, but it was not necessary for Burke to say *what* principles:

It is the business of the speculative philosopher to mark the proper ends of government. It is the business of the politician, who is the philosopher in action, to find out proper means towards those ends, and to employ them with effect. (ibid. 335)

Burke's contention was simply that to put any principles into effect, parity was needed. The whole case is argued pragmatically. The appeal is to history and observation, not to Natural Law. The only time a 'law of nature' is invoked, what is so described is an empirical generalisation: '... it is a law of nature, that whoever is necessary to what we have made our object, is sure in some way or in some time or other, to become our master' (ibid. 283–4).

Other empirical generalisations abound for instance:

It is true, that the peers have a great influence in the kingdom, and in every part of the publick concerns. While they are men of property, it is impossible to prevent it, except by such means as must prevent all property from its natural operation: an event not easily to be compassed, while property is power; nor by any means to be wished ××× (ibid. 245)

And an opening statement which looks like an affirmation of a democratic principle – 'in all disputes between them ['the people'] and their rulers, the presumption is at least upon a par in favour of the people' (ibid. 224) – turns out to be far short of that, for 'the people' are all those, but only those, who have enough property to make them an effective counterweight to the Court: they are 'the great peers, the leading landed gentlemen, the opulent merchants and manufacturers, the substantial yeomanry (ibid. 270).

Later, as we shall see, he defined 'the people' more precisely, both quantitatively – in England they amounted to about the upper 400,000 (RP 18.140–1) – and qualitatively – there is 'a people' only when they exist in an organic unity of orderly ranks (A 6.216) – but already his meaning is clear enough. A general moral principle, the rightful supremacy of the people is reduced to operational terms by a definition of the people drawn from Burke's bourgeois–aristocratic prejudices.

One of Burke's most often quoted principles comes from this same period, namely, his insistence, in his speech to the electors of Bristol, that a Member of Parliament is not an instructed delegate but a representative empowered to exercise his independent judgement:

Your representative owes you, not his industry only, but his judgment; and he betrays, instead of serving you, if he sacrifices it to your opinion.

... If government were a matter of will upon any side, yours, without question, ought to be superiour. But government and legislation are matters of reason and judgment, and not of inclination; and what sort of reason is that, in which the determination precedes the discussion; in which one set of men deliberate, and another decide; and where those who form the conclusion are perhaps three hundred miles distant from those who hear the arguments?

... Parliament is not a *congress* of ambassadors from different and hostile interests; which interests each must maintain, as an agent and advocate, against other agents and advocates; but parliament is a *deliberative* assembly of *one* nation, with *one* interest, that of the whole; where, not local purposes, not local prejudices ought to guide, but the general good, resulting from the general reason of the whole. You chuse a member indeed; but when you have chosen him, he is not a member of Bristol, but he is a member of *parliament.* (EB 3.19–20)

This commonsense principle, beloved of M.P.s ever since, was perfectly sensible at the time when M.P.s were not elected on clear party platforms. We cannot blame Burke for the use which has sometimes been made of that principle in later times, to excuse members elected on a specific party platform from living up to their commitments.

In the 1770s Burke was much taken up with British policy on America, attacking the arguments of government spokesmen and urging a more conciliatory policy. His speeches and writings on this are notable for their appeal to experience, as much as, or more than, to principle. He opened his *Speech on American Taxation* (given in the House of Commons in April 1774 and published in January 1775) with a demonstration from recent experience, that the repeal of the Stamp Act by the Rockingham ministry in 1766 had not led the colonists to demand repeal of any other taxes: hence the repeal of the tax on tea, a motion which Burke was supporting and the ministry was opposing, could not be opposed on that ground. The rest of the long speech is on the same ground of experience: it is a detailed analysis of the shifts in British policy since the fall of the Rockingham administration eight years before, and of the uniformly unfortunate consequences of those shifts.

Burke closed with an appeal to the House not to stand on its sovereign right to tax the colonies (a right which Burke never disputed), but to consider the consequences of exercising that right in the way they had recently done:

I am not here going into the distinctions of rights, nor attempting to mark their boundaries. I do not enter into these metaphysical distinctions; I hate the very sound of them.
. . . But if, intemperately, unwisely, fatally, you sophisticate and poison the very source of government, by urging subtle deductions, and consequences odious to those you govern, from the unlimited and illimitable nature of supreme sovereignty, you will teach them by these means to call that sovereignty itself in question. When you drive him hard, the boar will surely turn upon the hunters. (AT 2.432–3)

A year later, in the *Speech on Moving his Resolutions for Conciliation with the Colonies* (March 1775), he proceeds on the same grounds. He presents an array of facts about the American colonies, including the fact that the colonists were mainly Englishmen, devoted ever since the seventeenth-century emigration to the principle 'that in all monarchies the people must in effect themselves, mediately or immediately, possess the power of granting their own money, or no shadow of liberty could subsist (CC 3.51). That principle Burke fully endorses, but he does not urge it as a morally desirable principle: he simply cites the colonists' attachment to it as an experiential fact. It is in this context that he makes his oft-quoted remark: 'I do not know the method of drawing up an indictment against an whole people' (ibid. 69). And he insists that utility, in the broadest sense, should take precedence over legal right:

The question with me is, not whether you have a right to render your people miserable; but whether it is not your interest to make them happy. It is not, what a lawyer tells me, I *may* do; but what humanity, reason, and justice, tell me, I ought to do. (ibid. 75)

He closes with a last appeal against driving principles to their logical conclusion:

We Englishmen stop very short of the principles upon which we support any given part of our constitution; or even the' whole of it together.
. . . All government, indeed every human benefit and enjoyment, every virtue, and every prudent act, is founded on compromise and barter. We balance inconveniencies; we give and take; we remit some rights, that we may enjoy others; and, we choose rather to be happy citizens, than subtle disputants. (ibid. 110–11)

In all of this, as in the *Letter to the Sheriffs of Bristol on the Affairs of America* (1777) which we have already noticed, the appeal is not to principle but to the empirical fact of the colonists' attachment to a principle rooted in British history since at least the seventeenth century. There is no appeal to Natural Law, or to any universal principle other than utility in the broadest sense. The happiness of the people is the only criterion of policy, and how that is to be achieved can only be decided by painstaking attention to experience, to the fortunate and unfortunate consequences of various past governmental policies.

In 1780 Burke's attention turned back again to home affairs. The *Speech on Economical Reform*, as it is usually called, is not about economic policy but, as its full title indicates, is about reducing the statutory provision of money to the royal establishment: it is a *Speech on presenting to the House of Commons a Plan for the Better Security of the Independence of Parliament, and the Oeconomical Reformation of the Civil and Other Establishments*. It is a specific prescription to remedy the ill Burke had diagnosed ten years earlier in the *Thoughts on the Cause of the Present Discontents*, that is, that the large revenues given by Parliament to the Crown were being used to destroy the independence of Parliament. He holds up to ridicule the large number of now useless or redundant offices in the royal household (and in the separately-administered principalities, duchies etc. of Wales, Lancaster, Chester and Cornwall). All of these may have performed useful functions in feudal times; now their only use is to buy Members of Parliament by handing out these offices as sinecures. Burke's veneration of tradition does not extend that far: '... when the reason of old establishments is gone, it is absurd to preserve nothing but the burthen of them. This is superstitiously to embalm a carcass not worth an ounce of the gums that are used to preserve it' (ER 3.278). A previous attempt to reduce the charges of the King's table and kitchen had failed, Burke noted. 'Why? It was truly from a cause, which, though perfectly adequate to the effect, one would not have instantly guessed; – It was because the *turnspit in the king's kitchen was a member of parliament*' (ibid. 283).

Commonsense maxims based on experience are often propounded:

People will bear an old establishment when its excess is corrected, who will revolt at a new one. (ibid. 313)

An honourable and fair profit [from service to the state] is the best security against avarice and rapacity; as in all things else, a lawful and regulated enjoyment is the best security against debauchery and excess. For as wealth is power, so all power will infallibly draw wealth to itself by some means or other: and when men are left no way of ascertaining their profits but by their means of obtaining them, those means will be increased to infinity. (ibid. 316)

I know of no mode of preserving the effectual execution of any duty, but to make it the direct interest of the executive officer that it shall be faithfully performed. (ibid. 338)

Sometimes a principle distilled from experience is combined with a moral principle, as in his explanation of his refusal to recommend the abolition of any offices which 'have been considered as property':

What the law respects shall be sacred to me. If the barriers of law should be broken down, upon ideas of convenience, even of publick convenience, we shall have no longer anything certain among us. If the discretion of power is once let loose upon property, we can be at no loss to determine whose power, and what discretion it is that will prevail at last. (ibid. 308)

And again:

The people are the masters. They have only to express their wants at large and in gross. We are the expert artists; we are the skilful workmen, to shape their desires into perfect form, and to fit the utensil to the use. They are the sufferers, they tell the symptoms of the complaint; but we know the exact seat of the disease, and how to apply the remedy according to the rules of art. (ibid. 344)

And sometimes the moral principle, though very imprecisely stated, stands by itself: 'If I cannot reform with equity, I will not reform at all' (ibid 299).

Perhaps the most interesting general propositions are some, mentioned in passing as being self-evident, which reveal Burke's perception of the extent to which the market had become the determinant of all values, and his acceptance of an assumption which justified a policy of *laissez-faire*. To support his proposal that most of the services needed to maintain the royal household should be turned over to private enterprisers on a contractual basis, he observes:

The principles of trade have so pervaded every species of dealing, from the highest to the lowest objects; all transactions are got so much into system, that we may, at a moment's warning, and to a farthing value, be informed at what rate any service may be sup-plied. (ibid. 285)

And in speaking of the government's moribund Board of Trade and Plantations, 'which, if not mischievous, is of no use at all', he asks his hearers to

reflect how generally it is true, that commerce, the principal object of that office, flourishes most when it is left to itself. Interest, the great guide of commerce, is not a blind one. It is very well able to find its own way; and its necessities are its best laws. (ibid. 323)

The whole speech on economical reform, then, displays the same stance as is evident in his earlier work: the criterion of good measures and good institutions is the broadly utilitarian one of the general interest, which requires, beyond any doubt, the sanctity of property law. Given this end, the main thing is to attend to the most effective means: and that must be the work of the skilled men, the politicians, who must rely on analysis of the proven and probable effects of alternative policies.

During the 1780s most of Burke's energy was devoted to his crusade against the East India Company. England's Indian empire was indeed, in Burke's view, a proper white man's burden, but he took strong exception to the way Parliament had allowed that burden to be exercised, with inadequate oversight or control, by the chartered East India Company. He compiled such a mass of evidence of the Company's dishonourable, vicious, corrupt and genocidal behaviour, that he was able, almost single-handedly, to persuade the House of Commons to impeach the chief architect and defender of the Company's policies, Warren Hastings, and thereby to bring those policies into a glare of publicity unprecedented in British parliamentary history. His speeches and reports on India take up seven volumes of his sixteen-volume collected works, and he said, towards the end of his life (c 8.397–9; cf. NL 8.26) that he would rather be remembered for his efforts in defence of the Indian people than for anything else he had done.

What concerns us here is the extent to which Burke built his case against the Company, and for the impeachment of Hastings, on general principles of right. What we find is that he frequently invoked such general principles, but never defined them at all closely. He needed to invoke them: he knew he could not show that the Company's actions had been illegal, so his only recourse was to show that they offended against some more fundamental law. This law he sometimes described as divine, sometimes as natural, sometimes as moral. But he did not need to specify its content, for the activities of the Company and its servants, which Burke had put on record in enormous detail, were strikingly in defiance of the simplest principles of fairness and honesty.

In his *Speech on Fox's East India Bill*, (1 December 1783), he undertook to demonstrate three propositions about those activities and their results:

First . . . that there is not a *single* prince, state, or potentate, great or small, in India, with whom they have come into contact, whom they have not sold. I say *sold*, though sometimes they have not been able to deliver according to their bargain. Secondly, I say, that there is not a *single treaty* they have ever made, which they have not broken. Thirdly, I say, that there is not a single prince or state, who ever put any trust in the company, who is not utterly ruined; and that none are in any degree secure or flourishing, but in the exact proportion to their settled distrust and irreconcilable enmity to this nation. (EI 4.21)

Moreover, in the whole internal administration the rule of law had been replaced by arbitrary rule:

In effect, Sir, every legal regular authority in matters of revenue, of political administration, of criminal law, of civil law, in many of the most essential parts of military discipline, is laid level with the ground; and an oppressive, irregular, capricious, unsteady, rapacious, and peculating despotism, with a direct disavowal of obedience to any authority at home, and without any fixed maxim, principle, or rule of proceeding, to guide them in India, is at present the state of your charter-government over great kingdoms. (ibid. 93)

These charges, with the supporting evidence, were designed to show that the Company's behaviour was such an abuse of political power that its charter should not be renewed on the old terms.

Burke's major premise was that all political power is a trust. He asserted

that all political power which is set over men, and that all privilege claimed or exercised in exclusion of them, being wholly artificial, and for so much a derogation from the natural equality of mankind at large, ought to be some way or other exercised ultimately for their benefit.

... such rights or privileges, or whatever else you choose to call them, are all in the strictest sense a *trust*; and it is of the very essence of every trust to be rendered *accountable*; and even totally to *cease*, when it substantially varies from the purposes for which it alone could have a lawful existence. (ibid. 11)

This old Lockean Whig principle, rather than all the rhetorical appeals to Natural Law, was the logical basis of Burke's case for stripping the Company of its chartered privileges. It took care of the objection Burke foresaw would be made to his proposal, that is, that it was a confiscation of an established property right. He recognised that the Company's chartered rights were a property. But such 'chartered rights of men' as these were claimed to be must be subordinate to another sort of chartered rights of men, namely, those which (such as Magna Carta) confirm 'the natural rights of mankind'. Charters of the latter kind

have made the very name of a charter dear to the heart of every Englishman. But, Sir, there may be, and there are charters, not only different in nature, but formed on principles the *very reverse* of those of the great charter. Of this kind is the charter of the East-India company. Magna Charta is a charter to restrain power, and to destroy monopoly. The East-India charter is a charter to establish monopoly, and to create power. Political power and commercial monopoly are *not* the rights of men; and the rights of them derived from charters, it is fallacious and sophistical to call 'the chartered rights of men'. (ibid. 8–9)

This appeal from chartered rights to the natural rights of mankind is not at all inconsistent with Burke's later denigration, in the context of the French Revolution, of the 'rights of man': he is appealing here to such 'rights of men' as had been confirmed by old enactments. So he concludes:

> I ground myself therefore on this principle – that if the abuse is proved, the contract is broken; and we [i.e. Parliament] re-enter into all our rights; that is, into the exercise of all our duties: Our own authority is indeed as much a trust originally, as the company's authority is a trust derivatively; and it is the use we make of the resumed power that must justify or condemn us in the resumption of it. (ibid. 13)

In the actual impeachment proceedings, in which Burke was the spokesman of the Commons who brought the impeachment charges to the House of Lords, Burke led off from another Whig principle. His *Speech on Opening the Articles of Impeachment* (February 1788) begins by countering the principles on which Hastings, in earlier hearings, had defended his and the Company's activities. The most important of Hastings's principles was that the power which Parliament had delegated to the Company was sovereign power and hence absolute power. Burke acknowledged that sovereign power is by definition unaccountable to any higher legal body, and that sovereign power is necessary to govern any country. But he insisted that sovereign power could never be *arbitrary* power, because no people or legislature or executive could grant arbitrary power:

> *He* have arbitary power! My Lords, the East Indian Company have not arbitary power to give him; the King has no arbitrary power to give him; your Lordships have not; nor the Commons; nor the whole Legislature. We have no arbitrary power to give, because arbitrary power is a thing, which neither any man can hold nor any man can give. (01 13.165)

But instead of supporting the proposition that arbitrary power cannot be granted, as Locke had done, by a reasoned argument back to the natural rights of free and equal individuals, Burke flies directly to divine law:

We are all born in subjection, all born equally, high and low, governours and governed, in subjection to one great, immutable, pre-existent law, prior to all our devices, and prior to all our contrivances, paramount to all our ideas, and all our sensations, antecedent to our very existence, by which we are knit and connected in the eternal frame of the Universe, out of which we cannot stir.

This great law does not arise from our conventions or compacts; on the contrary, it gives to our conventions and compacts all the force and sanction they can have; – it does not arise from our vain institutions. Every good gift is of God; all power is of God; – and He, who has given the power, and from whom alone it originates, will never suffer the exercise of it to be practised upon any less solid foundation than the power itself. If then all dominion of man over man is the effect of the divine disposition, it is bound by the eternal laws of Him, that gave it, with which no human authority can dispense . . . (ibid. 165–6)

We are never told what this law is; the flight into rhetoric takes over.

Burke's style (so different from that of his mentor, Locke) has a great deal to answer for. Not least is that the difference of style is apt to distract our attention from a difference of substance. Locke had grounded the Whig case on the natural *rights* of dissociated individuals: Burke's Whig case is grounded on the divinely-ordained *duties* of persons born into submission. The logical line of Locke's thought, although often confused, was never dissolved into rhetorical flights. Burke's often was.

Burke's style is so much a part of his thinking that it deserves more than passing notice. Whether he deliberately developed that style in order to distract attention from logical deficiencies in his argument of which he was well aware, or whether his mind worked naturally on the dramatic and the logical level at the same time, is hard to say. Admirer as he was of the theatrical arts it is possible that he copied them unconsciously rather than deliberately, but there is no doubt that in his later writings, especially in the *Reflections*, he was a master of dramatic craft. Tom Paine, in his spirited reply, *Rights of Man*, remarked on this: he could 'consider Mr. Burke's book in scarcely any other light than a dramatic performance . . . omitting some facts, distorting others, and making the whole machinery bend to produce a stage effect.' Paine was even more concerned by what he considered to be Burke's deliberate efforts 'to lead his readers from the point by a wild, unsystematical display of paradoxical rhapsodies'. Burke's style was a necessary device: the style was the man. Paine writes:

It is not from his prejudices only, but from the disorderly cast of his genius, that he is unfitted for the subject he writes upon. Even his genius is without a constitution. It is a genius at random, and not a genius constituted. But he must say something. He has therefore mounted in the air like a balloon, to draw the eyes of the multitude from the ground they stand upon.

James Mackintosh, another contemporary critic, was even sharper. Fastening on the design of the *Reflections*, he wrote:

His subject is as extensive as political science — his allusions and excursions reach almost every region of human knowledge. It must be confessed that in this miscellaneous and desultory warfare, the superiority of a man of genius over common men is infinite. He can cover the most ignominious retreat by a brilliant allusion. He can parade his arguments with masterly generalship, where they are strong. He can escape from an untenable position into a splendid declamation. He can sap the most impregnable conviction by pathos, and put to flight a host of syllogisms with a sneer. Absolved from the laws of vulgar method, he can advance a groupe of magnificent horrors to make a breach in our hearts, through which the most undisciplined rabble of arguments may enter in triumph.

Paine was in little doubt, and Mackintosh in none at all, that Burke's style was a deliberate device to conceal the inadequacies of his logic.

Even Burke's staunchest nineteenth-century liberal admirer, John Morley, thought that Burke's style called for some apology:

The framework of what he has to say is too thickly overlaid with Asiatic ornament. His language burns with too consuming a blaze for the whole to diffuse that clear, undisturbed light which we are accustomed to find in men who have trained themselves to balance

ideas, to weigh mutually opposed speculations, in short, to argue and
to reason with no passion stronger than an intense desire to discover
on what side or on what sort of middle way the truth lies ... His
passion appears hopelessly fatal to anything like success in the pur-
suit of Truth, who does not reveal herself to followers thus inflamed.
His ornate style does not appear less fatal to that cautious and pre-
cise method of statement, suitable to matter which is not known at
all unless it is known distinctly.

This measured rebuke is no more than an expression of regret
that Burke's admirable empiricism had not brought him as far
as the scientific positivism of Comte, which Morley specifically
extolled in this context. Morley did not impute to Burke any
deliberate obfuscation: it was merely Burke's 'natural ardour'
that 'impelled him to clothe his conclusions in glowing and
exaggerated phrases'.

The twentieth-century reader will perhaps be more inclined
to share the view of Burke's critical contemporaries. Some more
evidence on which such a judgement can be based will appear
in the next chapter, where we shall notice Burke's flight into
rhetoric on the subject of the social contract. Here we may
simply notice that his rhetorical style was not confined to his
treatment of the French Revolution. It is found in his middle as
well as his late period, most often when he has recourse to
Natural Law or some other a priori principle.

Our digression on style may finish, as it began, with his
Indian speeches. Six years after his speech on opening the impeachment, his *Speech at the Close of the Impeachment* (1794)
concluded with another appeal to divine law, now given a new
edge by Burke's none too subtle reminder to the House of Lords
that in view of what the revolution in France had already done,
their own existence was now at risk. He pleaded that they
should at least go down with all flags flying:

My Lords, your House yet stands; it stands as a great edifice; but let
me say, that it stands in the midst of ruins; in the midst of the ruins,
that have been made by the greatest moral earthquake that ever
convulsed and shattered this globe of ours. My Lords, it has pleased
Providence to place us in such a state, that we appear every moment

to be upon the verge of some great mutations. There is one thing, and one thing only, which defies all mutation; that which existed before the world, and will survive the fabrick of the world itself; I mean justice; that justice, which, emanating from the Divinity, has a place in the breast of every one of us, given us for our guide with regard to ourselves, and with regard to others, and which will stand, after this globe is burned to ashes, our advocate or our accuser before the great Judge, when He comes to call upon us for the tenour of a well-spent life. (CI 16.417)

So ends what we may call Burke's middle period. It overlaps, as we have just noticed, his French Revolution period, and one might argue that it was his Indian crusade, rather than his French crusade, that first compelled him to appeal, against all his earlier inclinations, to a priori principles. The two crusades have indeed something in common. The intensity of the Indian crusade may well be attributed to his reverence for traditional establishments. Much of his case against the East India Company was that it had deliberately set out to destroy the ancient constitutions, laws and customs of all the proud kingdoms of the Indian sub-continent. He argued also that the Company's rule in India was already endangering the authority of the established propertied classes at home, by creating a despicable new breed of *nouveaux riches* who were bringing home untold plunder from their service in India.

Yet Burke's alarm about the French Revolution went deeper. He saw that the principles on which it was based would, if they were successfully exported, totally undermine the established order in England and the rest of Europe. They must therefore be countered by principles more substantive than those he had so far deployed. The English ruling class had until now treated Burke's principles as a paper tiger. Now he had to persuade them that the threat was real, and that it was an immediate threat to their whole way of life, that is, to their property. To do this he had to invest his divine and natural law with some property substance. He did not abandon his rhetoric – it even reached new heights – but now he backed it with some down-to-earth economic principles.

4 The Anglo-European wasp

Burke's most celebrated work, in his own time and ever since, is his *Reflections on the Revolution in France and on the Proceedings in Certain Societies in London Relative to that Event* (1790). The second part of his title should not be overlooked. It is highly significant. What concerned Burke most deeply was the foreseeable repercussions of the French Revolution in England, and then in the rest of Europe. The destruction of the old order in France, had it been confined to France, might have made Burke weep, but it would not have moved him to the measured argument of the *Reflections*, nor to the increasing fury of the writings of the last eight years of his life.

The reason for his concern is made quite explicit in 1790. Addressing himself to his French correspondent, he writes:

Formerly your affairs were your own concern only. We felt for them as men; but we kept aloof from them, because we were not citizens of France. But when we see the model held up to ourselves, we must feel as Englishmen, and feeling, we must provide as Englishmen. Your affairs, in spite of us, are made a part of our interest; so far at least as to keep at a distance your panacea, or your plague. If it be a panacea, we do not want it. We know the consequences of unnecessary physic. If it be a plague; it is such a plague, that the precautions of the most severe quarantine ought to be established against it. (R 185)

That quarantine required, as we shall see, more extensive pronouncements on the nature of society and government than any that had been required of Burke hitherto. It would be too much to say that Burke's writings of the 1790s contain a coherent political theory. There is no orderly development of a theory of political obligation or political right drawn from first principles of human nature, as with Hobbes and Locke. But there are the rudiments of such a general theory, and there is more about the nature of the British Constitution than in any of his earlier writings. Both were needed to counteract the 'armed doctrine' which Burke took the French Revolution to be, and especially to convince men of substance in Britain, some of whom were not unfriendly to the Revolution in its first stage, that its doctrine, if not exposed and rebutted, would undermine their whole way of life. The threat was not just to the Crown, the Established Church, and the aristocracy: it was also to men of property as a whole. For the French doctrine measured the claims of all those classes and institutions against an egalitarian principle, ultimately by denying their title to the property which sustained them. The sanctity of property, never far from Burke's thought, now took a more explicit place, and as we shall see this led him to say more about the political economy of the existing order than he had done before.

The rudiments of a general theory and a theory of the British Constitution are approached in the *Reflections* and more fully stated a year later in the *Appeal from the New to the Old Whigs*, which is a defence of the position he had taken in the *Reflections* and a spirited refutation of allegations that that position was a departure from the principles he had previously preached. We shall look at the *Reflections* and *Appeal* together. The political economy, also approached in those works, and more fully set out in the *Thoughts and Details on Scarcity* (1795), we shall examine in the next chapter.

In the *Reflections* Burke winds his way into his general principles by sustained praise of the principle of inheritance which he finds embodied in English charters and legislation from time immemorial. Countering the claim of the English friends of the new French principles that those principles were the principles of the Whig Revolution in England a century earlier, Burke has no difficulty citing chapter and verse to the contrary. He concludes, in a passage which deserves extended quotation, as showing how easily he could slide from an historical record to a transcendent principle said to inhere in the natural order of the universe:

You will observe, that from Magna Charta to the Declaration of Right, it has been the uniform policy of our constitution to claim and assert our liberties, as an *entailed inheritance* derived to us from our forefathers, and to be transmitted to our posterity, as an estate specially belonging to the people of this kingdom without any reference whatever to any other more general or prior right. By this means our constitution preserves an unity in so great a diversity of its parts. We have an inheritable crown; an inheritable peerage; and an house of commons and a people inheriting privileges, franchises, and liberties, from a long line of ancestors.

This policy appears to me to be the result of profound reflection; or rather the happy effect of following nature, which is wisdom without reflection, and above it. A spirit of innovation is generally the result of a selfish temper and confined views. People will not look forward to posterity, who never look backward to their ancestors. Besides, the people of England well know, that the idea of inheritance furnishes a sure principle of conservation, and a sure principle of transmission; without at all excluding a principle of improvement. It leaves acquisition free; but it secures what it acquires. Whatever advantages are obtained by a state proceeding on these maxims, are locked fast as in a sort of family settlement; grasped as in a kind of mortmain for ever. By a constitutional policy, working after the pattern of nature, we receive, we hold, we transmit our government and our privileges, in the same manner in which we enjoy and transmit our property and our lives. The institutions of policy, the goods of fortune, the gifts of Providence, are handed down, to us and from us, in the same course and order. Our political system is placed in a just correspondence and symmetry with the order of the world, and with the mode of existence decreed to a permanent body composed of transitory parts . . . (R 119–20)

There is no theoretical basis for this praise of inheritance except the rough utilitarian one that institutions which have lasted a long time have thereby demonstrated their utility. Burke's presumption in favour of old institutions was a long-standing one. His opposition to any reform of the franchise at home had always been based on it. He recognised that the strong case, indeed the only case, against reform lay in that presumption, as in his 1782 speech on reform:

. . . our Constitution is a prescriptive Constitution; it is a Constitution, whose sole authority is, that it has existed time out of mind

... Prescription is the most solid of all titles, not only to property, but, which is to secure that property, to Government. They harmonize with each other, and give mutual aid to one another. It is accompanied with another ground of authority in the constitution of human mind, presumption. It is a presumption in favour of any settled scheme of government against any untried project, that a nation has long existed and flourished under it. It is a better presumption even of the *choice* of a nation, far better than any sudden and temporary arrangement by actual election. Because a nation is not an idea only of local extent, and individual momentary aggregation, but it is an idea of continuity, which extends in time as well as in numbers, and in space. And this is a choice not of one day, or one set of people, not a tumultuary or giddy choice; it is a deliberate election of ages and of generations, it is a Constitution made by what is ten thousand times better than choice ... Nor is prescription of government formed upon blind unmeaning prejudices – for man is a most unwise, and a most wise, being. The individual is foolish. The multitude, for the moment, is foolish, when they act without deliberation; but the species is wise, and when time is given to it, as a species it almost always acts right. (RCP 10.96–7)

The sentiment is clear, though the logic is not. If no single momentary choice has any standing, what standing has any protracted series of momentary choices? If the idea is that small incremental changes are admissible, how small must they be? What is the distinction between the multitude, which may be foolish, and the species, which is almost always wise? The answer to the last question we shall find in the *Appeal*, as quoted below (at A 6.216). Here we need only notice how his case for prescription as not based on 'blind unmeaning prejudices' supports his preference in the *Reflections* for prejudice over reason:

We know that *we* have made no discoveries; and we think that no discoveries are to be made, in morality; nor many in the great principles of government, nor in the ideas of liberty, which were understood long before we were born, altogether as well as they will be after the grave has heaped its mould upon our presumption, and the silent tomb shall have imposed its law on our pert loquacity.
... I am bold enough to confess, that we are generally men of

untaught feelings; that instead of casting away all our old prejudices, we cherish them to a very considerable degree, and, to take
more shame to ourselves, we cherish them because they are prejudices,
and the longer they have lasted, and the more generally they have
prevailed, the more we cherish them. We are afraid to put men to
live and trade each on his own private stock of reason; because we
suspect that this stock in each man is small, and the individuals
would do better to avail themselves of the general bank and capital of
nations, and of ages. (R 182–3)

Burke's recommendation of prejudice as performing the same
function in politics as capital does in the economic life of a
nation is a nice touch. The mercantile analogy came as naturally to his mind here as it had done sixty pages earlier, when
he summarised his complaint that the French had thrown away
all the valuable elements in their old constitution, on which he
thought they ought to have built their reformation, in the tell-
ing sentence: 'You set up your trade without a capital' (R 122).

The core of Burke's theory comes when he deduces the essence of civil society from his view of human nature and hence
of the 'natural' condition of mankind. Burke was ahead of his
time in seeing that the state of nature from which Locke had
had his men move into civil society was virtually the same as
Hobbes's 'natural condition of mankind', that is, a condition in
which man's appetites would lead them to such strife that no
one's person or property could be secure. If Burke's argument
seems a nice blend of Hobbes and Locke, it leans more to
Hobbes. Men do not enter into civil society in order to protect
their natural rights: on entering civil society they must give up
their natural rights, which are 'absolutely repugnant' to it
(R 150). They are repugnant because, out of civil society, there
is no sufficient restraint on men's passions:

Society requires not only that the passions of individuals should be
subjected, but that even in the mass and body as well as in the
individuals, the inclinations of men should frequently be thwarted,
their will controlled, and their pasions brought into subjection. This
can only be done *by a power out of themselves*; and not, in the
exercise of its function, subject to that will and to those passions
which it is its office to bridle and subdue. (R 151)

The point is made again in the *Letter to a Member of the National Assembly* (1791):

Society cannot exist unless a controuling power upon will and appetite be placed somewhere, and the less of it there is within [the average citizen], the more there must be without. It is ordained in the eternal constitution of things, that men of intemperate minds cannot be free. Their passions forge their fetters. (NA 6.64)

Here is the Leviathan state indeed: not merely individual men but the whole mass must be 'brought into subjection'.

But Burke saw no problem here, for he held that men, being now born into civil society, and enjoying its advantages, must be presumed to have agreed to that subjection. And it was not onerous so long as it was imposed only through traditional institutions to which people had become accustomed. So the argument comes full circle: inherited rights are the only real rights of man. His catalogue of 'the *real* rights of man' is revealing:

Men have a right to live by that rule [the rule of law]; they have a right to justice; as between their fellows, whether their fellows are in politic function or in ordinary occupation. They have a right to the fruits of their industry; and to the means of making their industry fruitful. They have a right to the acquisitions of their parents; to the nourishment and improvement of their offspring; to instruction in life, and to consolation in death. Whatever each man can separately do, without trespassing upon others, he has a right to do for himself; and he has a right to a fair portion of all which society, with all its combinations of skill and force, can do in his favour. In this partnership all men have equal rights; but not to equal things. He that has but five shillings in the partnership, has as good a right to it, as he that has five hundred pounds has to his larger proportion. But he has not a right to an equal dividend in the product of the joint stock; and as to the share of power, authority, and direction which each individual ought to have in the management of the state, that I must deny to be amongst the direct original rights of men in civil society; for I have in my contemplation the civil social man, and no other. It is a thing to be settled by convention. (R 149–50)

The catalogue of the real rights of man moves from the most

general right to the protection of the law, or justice as against officials and fellow-subjects, through a right to the fruits of one's labour and to inherited accumulations, to a right to religious consolation. The catalogue ends with an assertion of a joint-stock principle of material entitlements: each man is entitled to a share of the whole social product proportional to what he has contributed to its production. And it is evident that the contribution is of inherited capital as well as of labour, for in Burke's numerical example (5 shillings to 500 pounds) the ratio of contributions is 1:2,000, a range scarcely to be accounted for as a difference in labour inputs.

This dismissal of the French 'rights of man', however, left another question which Burke had to deal with: may the people, whose consent must be understood to have authorised civil society and the existing frame of government, ever reclaim their original right to establish whatever form of government they pleased? This led Burke into another circular argument. They could rightly do so only if they were constituted as a people, rather than being a mere aggregation of individuals. And they could only be counted as 'a people' if they had already accepted a hierarchical order:

In a state of *rude* nature there is no such thing as a people. A number of men in themselves have no collective capacity. The idea of a people is the idea of a corporation. It is wholly artificial; and made like all other legal fictions by common agreement ... When men, therefore, break up the original compact or agreement which gives its corporate form and capacity to a state, they are no longer a people ... They are a number of vague loose individuals, and nothing more. (A 6.210–11)

To enable men to act with the weight and character of a people, and to answer the ends for which they are incorporated into that capacity, we must suppose them (by means immediate or consequential) to be in that state of habitual social discipline, in which the wiser, the more expert, and the more opulent conduct, and by conducting enlighten and protect the weaker, the less knowing, and the less provided with the goods of fortune. When the multitude are not under this discipline, they can scarcely be said to be in civil society. (A 6.216)

This concept of civil society and of 'the people' gives short shrift to the French rights of man:

The pretended *rights of man* ... cannot be the rights of the people. For to be a people, and to have these rights, are things incompatible. The one supposes the presence, the other the absence of a state of civil society. (A 6.234)

Burke was quite willing to see civil society as a contract, but of a very odd sort: it was between three sets of people, two of whom were non-existent.

Society is indeed a contract. Subordinate contracts for objects of mere occasional interests may be dissolved at pleasure – but the state ought not to be considered as nothing better than a partnership agreement in a trade of pepper and coffee, callico or tobacco, or some other such low concern, to be taken up for a little temporary interest, and to be dissolved by the fancy of parties. It is to be looked on with other reverence; because it is not a partnership in things subservient only to the gross animal existence of a temporary and perishable nature. It is a partnership in all science; a partnership in all art; a partnership in every virtue, and in all perfection. As the ends of such a partnership cannot be obtained in many generations, it becomes a partnership not only between those who are living, but between those who are living, those who are dead, and those who are to be born. Each contract of each particular state is but a clause in the great primaeval contract of eternal society, linking the lower with the higher natures, connecting the visible and the invisible world, according to a fixed compact sanctioned by the inviolable oath which holds all physical and all moral natures, each in their appointed place. This law is not subject to the will of those, who by an obligation above them, and infinitely superior, are bound to submit their will to that law. The municipal corporations of that universal kingdom are not morally at liberty at their pleasure, and on their speculations of a contingent improvement, wholly to separate and tear asunder the bands of their subordinate community, and to dissolve it into an unsocial, uncivil, unconnected chaos of elementary principles. (R 194–5)

Here again Burke's flight into rhetoric takes the place of a reasoned discussion. He raises in one sentence a question largely neglected by the eighteenth-century rationalists: what obligations have we to future generations? How should we balance our rights against theirs? This is a question much to the forefront in the late twentieth century, as we become conscious of the reckless use we are making of non-renewable natural resources, and our equally reckless disregard of the inescapable by-products of our shining new resource, nuclear energy. Burke could not have foreseen our present predicament, but one might have expected some discussion of the general principle; instead we are given 'the great primaeval contract of eternal society' and the rest. In so far as the rhetoric bears analysis at all, it may be said to swing the question backwards rather than forward. His concern is that *old* rights should not be denied or uprooted, but be sustained for the enjoyment of the present and future generations. This takes us no further than the case we have already seen for prescriptive and inherited rights: it leaves untouched the question of the content of those rights.

Burke's concept of civil society leads easily into his theory of representation. In the first place, simple majority rule has no standing:

Out of civil society nature knows nothing of it; nor are men even when arranged according to civil order, otherwise than by very long training, brought at all to submit to it. . . . This mode of decision . . . must be the result of a very particular and special convention, confirmed afterwards by long habits of obedience, by a sort of discipline in society, and by a strong hand, vested with stationary permanent power, to enforce this sort of constructive general will. (A 6.212–3)

Burke goes on to point out that some contemporary states require, to validate some of their acts, a proportion of voices greater than a simple majority, and for other acts less than that. It is entirely a matter of convention, not natural right, and can only be decided by a disciplined people:

. . . to come to particulars, it is equally clear, that neither in France nor in England has the original, or any subsequent compact of the state, expressed or implied, constituted *a majority of men, told by the head,* to be the acting people of their several communities. (A 6.215–6)

Not only was there no case in compact or convention for majority rule: the presumption was against it even on general utilitarian grounds, because the many do not always know what is in their own interest. 'The will of the many, and their interest, must very often differ' (R 141).

How, then, should the general interest be represented? The first thing on which Burke insisted was that large property should be represented out of all proportion to the number of its holders.

Nothing is a due and adequate representation of a state, that does not represent its ability, as well as its property. But as ability is a vigorous and active principle, and as property is sluggish, inert, and timid, it can never be safe from the invasions of ability, unless it be, out of all proportion, predominant in the representation. It must be represented too in great masses of accumulation, or it is not rightly protected. The characteristic essence of property, formed out of the combined principles of its acquisition and conversation, is to be *unequal.* The great masses therefore which excite envy, and tempt rapacity, must be put out of the possibility of danger. Then they form a natural rampart about the lesser properties in all their gradations. . . . The plunder of the few would indeed give but a share inconceivably small in the distribution to the many. But the many are not capable of making this calculation . . . (R 140)

This principle was perfectly consistent with Burke's call for rule by a 'natural aristocracy', for the members of such a body, which Burke refused to regard as a class – 'a true natural aristocracy is not a separate interest in the state, or separable from it' (A 6.217) – had to be people of substantial property. They were mainly the nobility and gentry, who were leisured and educated and were bred to a sense of *noblesse oblige,* but they included also men of law, of science and of the arts, and 'rich traders, who from their success are presumed to have sharp and vigorous understandings, and to possess the virtues of diligence, order, constancy, and regularity, and to have cultivated an habitual regard to commutative justice' (A 6.218). All of these ought to take 'the leading, guiding and governing part' in society: to treat them merely as so many units 'is a horrible usurpation' (A 6.218–9).

The whole class entitled to the franchise was not much larger. Burke gave a rough estimate of its size:

In England and Scotland I compute that those of adult age, not declining in life, of tolerable leisure for such discussions, and of some means of information, more, or less, and who are above menial dependence, (or what is virtually such) may amount to about four hundred thousand. There is such a thing as a natural representative of the people. This body is that representative; and on this body, more than on the legal constituent, the artificial representative depends. This is the British publick; and it is a publick very numerous. The rest, when feeble, are the objects of protection; when strong, the means of force. (RPI 8.140–41)

This 'publick' corresponded well enough to the existing franchise:

... our representation has been found perfectly adequate to all the purposes for which a representation of the people can be desired or devised. I defy the enemies of our constitution to shew the contrary. (R 146)

There are one or two apparent discrepancies in Burke's treatment of representation but they are not substantial. In the *Reflections* he upbraids the French for having thrown over 'the elements of a constitution very nearly as good as could be wished'.

In your old states ... you had all that combination, and all that opposition of interests, you had that action and counteraction which, in the natural and in the political world, from the reciprocal struggle of discordant powers, draws out the harmony of the universe. These opposed and conflicting interests, which you considered as so great a blemish in your old and our present constitution, interpose a salutary check to all precipitate resolutions; They render deliberation a matter not of choice, but of necessity; they make all change a subject of *compromise*, which naturally begets moderation ... (R 122)

This praise of a constitution which sets the opposed interests of the different orders or classes against each other does not sit well with his case for 'virtual representation', which assumes that there is no difference of class interests:

Virtual representation is that in which there is a communion of interests, and a sympathy in feelings and desires between those who act in the name of any description of people, and the people in whose name they act, though the trustees are not actually chosen by them. This is virtual representation. Such a representation I think to be, in many cases, even better than the actual. It possesses most of its advantages, and is free from many of its inconveniences ... (HL 6.360)

That was written in 1792. By 1796 Burke admitted that the English were a divided people, but he did not see this as a class division: it was a division between those members of the ruling class who had been deluded by the Jacobins and those who had not, but who were so disposed to peace that they would not support Burke's demand for an all-out war against France (RPI 8.140–43). Burke was consistent to the end: the people were never divided except when some of them were misled. The case for virtual rather than actual representation of the many was untouched.

Indeed, even his recommendation that discordant powers should be constitutionally set off against each other is made on the ground that this draws out a natural harmony: 'in the natural and in the political world ... the reciprocal struggle of discordant powers, draws out the harmony of the universe' (R 122). Burke has read into the universe a harmony underlying opposed motions, and has read it back out into the real world as a constitutional principle. How did he come by this harmonious view of the universe? Clearly it has much in common with the medieval Christian Natural Law concept, so that it is plausible to attribute his position, as one school of his interpreters has done, to his acceptance of, and repeated insistence on, the

Christian Natural Law. But to rest the explanation there is to overlook the fact that Burke had put a quite different content into his natural law. It is a social and economic content, which can only have been derived from his reading of his own contemporary society. To see this we must turn to Burke's political economy.

5 The bourgeois political economist

We have already noticed that Burke was a close student of economic affairs and commercial policy from early on in his political career. He took that to be part of his duty as a Member of Parliament, and there is plenty of evidence of his industry in that regard, notably the detailed economic analysis of the *Observations* (1769). He recommended himself to his Bristol constituency in the 1770s partly on the ground of his knowledge of commercial principles. His case for a more lenient British policy towards the American colonies, and towards Ireland, and his sustained attack on the East India Company, were similarly based. He boasted, after he had left Parliament, of how much he had done 'in the way of political oeconomy' as an M.P. and even before that, claiming that the pension he had been awarded after his retirement would have been justified if he had been considered 'only as an oeconomist':

> If I had not deemed it of some value, I should not have made political oeconomy an object of my humble studies, from my very early youth to near the end of my service in parliament, even before (at least to any knowledge of mine) it had employed the thoughts of speculative men in other parts of Europe. At that time it was still in its infancy in England, where, in the last century it had its origin. Great and learned men thought my studies were not wholly thrown away, and deigned to communicate with me now and then on some particulars of their immortal works. Something of these studies may appear incidentally in some of the earliest things I published. The house has been witness to their effect, and has profited of them more or less, for above eight and twenty years. (NL 8.27)

We have noticed, too, that Burke had not only the narrow skill of an analyst of economic policy but also some grasp of broad principles of *political* economy, of the underlying importance of economic class relations (as in the *Vindication* and the *Tract on the Popery Laws*) and of the way in which market relations had penetrated social and political relations (as in the *Economical Reform*). But it was not until the threat from the French Revolution had compelled Burke to embark on some more general theory that he permitted himself anything like a full statement of his assumptions about political economy. His fullest statement of them then, in the *Thoughts and Details on Scarcity* (1795), was in response to an additional threat he saw to the established order at home, but he took that threat back to the same false principles he saw underlying the French Revolutionary policies.

The new threat was the spectre of Speenhamland. The Justices of the Peace in Speenhamland, Berkshire, not far from Burke's estate of six hundred acres in the adjoining county of Buckinghamshire, had that year put into effect a system of payments to labourers supplementary to wages, on a scale related to the size of the labourer's family and the cost of bread. They had done this in response to the acute distress of the labourers, whose wages were then below a subsistence level. Burke was afraid that the government might make this a national policy, and he wrote to urge them not to do so. Any such action would be both useless and wicked: it would dry up the springs of enterprise, which would leave the labourers even worse off; and this is because it would be an unnatural and impious interference with the laws of the market, and an arbitrary tax on property (s 7.380). It could be contemplated as an effective relief of the poor only by men ignorant or forgetful of the laws of political economy. Burke wrote to inform or remind such men of those laws, and of the necessary connection of those laws with the defence of property and hence of civilisation. The argument is based on the same economic assumptions as those of the *Reflections* five years earlier and the *Regicide Peace* a year or two later.

To see how central to Burke's political theory were his bourgeois assumptions about the actual and the desirable economic order, we may look first at his evident predilection for a freely competitive market economy, and then at his more fundamental assumption, which is less often noticed, that the market whose naturalness, necessity and justice he was celebrating was a specifically capitalist one.

Burke's preference in the matter of commercial policy was always for free trade, provided that diplomatic and strategic considerations did not call for some abatement from that principle, as he thought they did in the case of the English Navigation Acts. International commerce could, and when feasible and desirable should, be an instrument of economic warfare. Commercial treaties, as with France in 1787, should be made not on short-run grounds of immediate economic advantage, but on long-run grounds of their probable effect in weakening or strengthening a rival nation. Burke's position on this, arrived at independently, coincided with Adam Smith's proviso about *laissez-faire*: defence is more important than opulence.

But about the virtue of *laissez-faire* at home Burke had no doubts. A competitive, self-regulating market economy was the ideal. It was the most efficient system of production. It was the most equitable system of distribution of the whole product. It was a necessary part of the natural order of the universe. It was, even, divinely ordained, which set the seal on its being both necessary and equitable.

The system Burke saw as natural and necessary, and praised as efficient and equitable, was not a simple market economy in which independent small producers – peasants and craftsmen – exchanged their products to mutual advantage. It was a specifically capitalist economy. The motor of his system was the desire for accumulation. The mechanism was the employment of wage–labour by capital so as to yield a profit to the capitalist. It was *this* system that Burke held to be natural, necessary and equitable. The evidence for this is clear, though not often noticed or given much weight by Burke's admirers. Only after we have examined it will we be in a position to appreciate his extraordinary theoretical achievement.

The desire to accumulate, which Burke took to be natural, at least in those who had some capital already, was the source of every state's prosperity:

Monied men ought to be allowed to set a value on their money; if they did not, there could be no monied men. This desire of accumulation, is a principle without which the means of their service to the state could not exist. The love of lucre, though sometimes carried to a ridiculous, sometimes to a vicious excess, is the grand cause of prosperity to all states. In this natural, this reasonable, this powerful, this prolifick principle ... it is for the statesman to employ it as he finds it, with all its concomitant excellencies, with all its imperfections on its head. It is his part, in this case, as it is in all other cases, where he is to make use of the general energies of nature, to take them as he finds them. (RP3 8.354)

There is nothing the matter with avarice: the more avaricious the employer is, the more he must take care of his labourers:

But if the farmer is excessively avaricious? – why so much the better – the more he desires to increase his gains, the more interested is he in the good condition of those, upon whose labour his gains must principally depend. (S 7.385)

Burke had not changed his position in the thirty years since he first described avarice as laudable because it led to capital accumulation and the wealth of the nation (P 9.387), as cited above in Chapter 3, p. 21.

Burke took it as self-evident that the capitalists' income came from the surplus produced by the actual producers, and he saw this as beneficial to the community provided that the surplus was ploughed back into production. Speaking, as he so often did, of the landed capitalists (the kind he knew best, since he was one himself, but who operated no differently from any others), he wrote:

In every prosperous community something more is produced than goes to the immediate support of the producer. This surplus forms the income of the landed capitalist. It will be spent by a proprietor who does not labour. But this idleness is itself the spring of labour; this repose the spur to industry. The only concern of the state is, that the capital taken in rent from the land, should be returned again to the industry from whence it came ... (R 270)

He was clear that the rich lived off the labour of the poor, but held that, for two reasons, this was no ground for redistributing wealth. For one thing, a wholesale redistribution would give each of the poor an insignificant amount. More important, it would dry up the springs of wealth.

. . . all the classes and descriptions of the rich . . . are the pensioners of the poor, and are maintained by their superfluity. They are under an absolute, hereditary, and indefeasible dependence on those who labour, and are miscalled the poor.

The labouring people are only poor, because they are numerous. Numbers in their nature imply poverty. In a fair distribution among a vast multitude, none can have much. That class of dependent pensioners called the rich, is so extremely small, that if all their throats were cut, and a distribution made of all they consume in a year, it would not give a bit of bread and cheese for one night's supper to those who labour, and who in reality feed both the pensioners and themselves.

But the throats of the rich ought not to be cut, nor their magazines plundered; because, in their persons they are trustees for those who labour, and their hoards are the banking-houses of these latter. Whether they mean it or not, they do, in effect, execute their trust . . . (s 7.376–7)

Burke had no patience with modish talk about 'the labouring poor', nor with plans for the relief of the able-bodied poor:

Hitherto the name of poor (in the sense in which it is used to excite compassion) has not been used for those who can, but for those who cannot labour – for the sick and infirm; for orphan infancy; for languishing and decrepid age: but when we affect to pity as poor, those who must labour or the world cannot exist, we are trifling with the condition of mankind. (RP3 8.368)

Not only must the able-bodied poor work, to keep the world going: they must do so, Burke held, as wage-labourers, selling their labour as a commodity for a wage determined by impersonal market forces. That was necessary because that was the source of the profit which was the source of the capital which kept the world going. In Burke's view, as we shall now see, the wage relation was not only necessary but also natural, and therefore equitable.

Burke did not always distinguish between the capitalist as a mere receiver of interest or rent and the capitalist as a risk-taking enterpriser, but he was clear that the mainspring of the whole productive system was the profit to be made by employing wage-labour, which must be treated simply as a commodity in the market:

Labour is a commodity like every other, and rises or falls according to the demand. This is in the nature of things ... (s 7.379)

The demand depends on the employer's ability to make a profit from the employment of wage-labour:

There is an implied contract, much stronger than any instrument or article of agreement between the labourer in any occupation and his employer – that the labour ... shall be sufficient to pay to the employer a profit on his capital, and a compensation for his risk. (s 7.380)

Wages must, in the nature of things, depend on market supply and demand. Since labour is a commodity, 'and as such, an article of trade',

then labour must be subject to all the laws and principles of trade, and not to regulation foreign to them, and that may be totally inconsistent with those principles and those laws. When any commodity is carried to market, it is not the necessity of the vender, but the necessity of the purchaser that raises the price. The extreme want of the seller has rather (by the nature of things with which we shall in vain contend) the direct contrary operation ... The impossibility of the subsistence of a man, who carries his labour to a market, is totally beside the question ... The only question is, what is it worth to the buyer? (s 7.386)

The market in labour is like every other commodity market; it is governed by natural laws which the state cannot effectively contravene. If the state attempts to raise wages above the market rate, it is no help to the wage-earner:

If a commodity is raised by authority above what it will yield with a profit to the buyer, that commodity will be the less dealt in. If ... an attempt is made to force the purchase of the commodity (of labour for instance), the one of these two things must happen, either that the forced buyer is ruined, or the price of the product of the labour, in that proportion is raised. Then the wheel turns round, and the evil complained of falls with aggravated weight on the complainant. (S 7.387)

Burke asserted that the wage-earner had not done too badly in recent years in England, backing this assertion with first-hand evidence from his own observation:

If the happiness of the animal man (which certainly goes somewhere towards the happiness of the rational man) be the object of our estimate, then I assert without the least hesitation, that the condition of those who labour (in all descriptions of labour, and in all gradations of labour, from the highest to the lowest inclusively) is on the whole extremely meliorated, if more and better food is any standard of melioration. (S 7.378)

He went into considerable detail about the fortunes of several subdivisions of that wage-earning class which he knew at first hand, namely the agricultural wage-earners, or 'labourers in husbandry' (S 7.388–90): all of them were doing well enough.

But the principle on which he was most insistent was, that in those years when the market did not treat the wage-earners well, even to the point that wages were less than bare subsistence, the state should not intervene:

But what if the rate of hire to the labourer comes far short of his necessary subsistence, and the calamity of the time is so great as to threaten actual famine? Is the poor labourer to be abandoned to the flinty heart and griping hand of base self-interest, supported by the sword of law, especially when there is reason to suppose that the very avarice of farmers themselves has concurred with the errours of government to bring famine on the land?

In that case, my opinion is this. Whenever it happens that a man can claim nothing according to the rules of commerce, and the principles of justice, he passes out of that department, and comes within the jurisdiction of mercy. In that province the magistrate has nothing at all to do: his interference is a violation of the property which it is his office to protect. (S 7.390–1)

State regulation of wages or intervention in the labour market, then, was not only useless but was also unjust. It was 'the rules of commerce' that were 'the principles of justice'. Burke's distributive justice, like Hobbes's a century and a half earlier, was the justice of the market. Burke put the same point positively, and referred it to common observation:

Nobody, I believe, has observed with any reflexion what market is, without being astonished at the truth, the correctness, the celerity, the general equity, with which the balance of wants is settled. (S 7.398)

Burke took this notion of the necessity and hence equity of the capitalist market to an extraordinary length. He knew that that order condemned many of the working class to a subhuman existence, but that had to be allowed in the interests of 'the great wheel of circulation', as in his reference to those who work

from dawn to dark in the innumerable servile, degrading, unseemly, unmanly, and often most unwholesome and pestiferous occupations, to which by the social oeconomy so many wretches are inevitably doomed. If it were not generally pernicious to disturb the natural course of things, and to impede, in any degree, the great wheel of circulation which is turned by the strangely directed labour of these unhappy people, I should be infinitely more inclined forcibly to rescue them from their miserable industry . . . I am sure that no consideration, except the necessity of submitting to the yoke of luxury, and the despotism of fancy, who in their own imperious way will distribute the surplus product of the soil, can justify the toleration of such trades and employments in a well-regulated state. (R 271)

But such an arrangement had to be tolerated: its victims could not be rescued from 'the natural course of things'.

Generally, however, Burke took a more sanguine view of the position of the wage-earner, partly on the empirical grounds we have already noticed, but fundamentally on a providential view of the universe. If things were hard on the labourer, as they sometimes were, that was simply a temporary incident in the working of a divinely-ordained natural order. It is the duty of governments and of all thinking men manfully to resist the very first idea, speculative or practical, that it is within the competence of government, taken as government, or even of the rich, as rich, to supply to the poor, those necessaries which it has pleased the Divine Providence for a while to with-hold from them. We, the people, ought to be made sensible, that it is not in breaking the laws of commerce, which are the laws of nature, and consequently the laws of God, that we are to place our hope of softening the Divine displeasure to remove any calamity under which we suffer, or which hangs over us. (S 7.404)

Whatever one may think of Burke's theology, one need not doubt his certainty that the laws of the market were divinely ordained. Nor need one doubt that it was because of his political economy that he found no difficulty in accepting that ordination, and recommending it to his readers. The central assumption of his political economy is strikingly like Adam Smith's 'invisible hand', though Burke's assumption is more obtrusively theological:

the benign and wise Disposer of all things . . . obliges men, whether they will or not, in pursuing their own selfish interests, to connect the general good with their own individual success. (S 7.384–5)

The natural order is harmonious:

nothing but the malignity, perverseness, and ill-governed passions of mankind, and particularly the envy they bear to each other's prosperity, could prevent their seeing and acknowledging it . . . (S 7.384)

The immediate conclusion from this was of course that the state should not attempt to intervene in the market, especially not to interfere with market wages rates:

Let government protect and encourage industry, secure property, repress violence, and discountenance fraud, it is all that they have to do. In other respects, the less they meddle in these affairs the better; the rest is in the hands of our Master and theirs. (RP3 8.367)

Burke's paradigm case was the relation between the employing farmer and the agricultural labourer. The relation he saw was a curious blend of free contract and customary status, and this brings us close to the heart of his vision of the social universe. The interests of the employing farmer and the labourer were identical: their contracts could not be onerous to either, for if they were, the contracts would not be made:

… in the case of the farmer and the labourer, their interests are always the same, and it is absolutely impossible that their free contracts can be onerous to either party. It is in the interest of the farmer, that his work should be done with effect and celerity: and that cannot be, unless the labourer is well fed, and otherwise found with such necessaries of animal life, according to his habitudes, as may keep the body in full force, and the mind gay and cheerful. (s 7.383)

But this identity of interests operated only because the wage relation was part of a natural chain of subordination, which Burke, following his beloved ancient writers, saw as extending from the employing farmer, through his human employees, to his cattle, and finally to his ploughs and spades:

… of all the instruments of his [the farmer's] trade, the labour of man (what the antient writers have caled the *instrumentum vocale*) is that on which he is most to rely for the repayment of his capital. The other two, the *semivocale* in the antient classification, that is, the working stock of cattle, and the *instrumentum mutum*, such as carts, ploughs, spades, and so forth, though not all inconsiderable in themselves, are very much inferiour in utility or in expence; or without a given portion of the first, are nothing at all. For in all things whatever, the mind is the most valuable and the most important; and in this scale the whole of agriculture is in a natural and just order; the beast is as an informing principle to the plough and cart; the labourer is as reason to the beast; and the farmer is as a thinking and presiding principle to the labourer. An attempt to break this chain of subordination in any part is equally absurd … (s 7.383–4)

The mutual advantage of the farmer and the labourer depends on their acceptance of this natural and just chain of subordination.

This is but a particular case of a more general rule which Burke had laid down in the *Reflections*, a rule which is the heart of his political economy. Speaking there of the need for capital accumulation, which as we have already seen was the starting-point of his political economy, he wrote:

> To be enabled to acquire, the people, without being servile, must be tractable and obedient. The magistrate must have his reverence, the laws their authority. The body of the people must not find the principles of natural subordination by art rooted out of their minds. They must respect that property of which they cannot partake. They must labour to obtain what by labour can be obtained; and when they find, as they commonly do, the success disproportioned to the endeavour, they must be taught their consolation in the final proportions of eternal justice. Of this consolation, whoever deprives them, deadens their industry, and strikes at the root of all acquisition as of all conservation. He that does this is the cruel oppressor ... (R 372)

With this we have the crucial point of Burke's political economy. Accumulation is essential. It is possible only if the body of the people accept a subordination which generally shortchanges them. That subordination is natural and customary: the common people will accept it if they are not seduced by art. It is right that they should accept it, for it is in tune with 'the final proportions of eternal justice'. The seductive art that Burke feared was of course the egalitarian propaganda of the French revolutionists and their English supporters, which would undo the whole fabric of the natural, customary and just social order of subordination of ranks.

Everyone sees that Burke had always been a defender of a traditional, inherited social order of subordination of ranks. What has not generally been seen is that the traditional order which he cherished was not simply any hierarchical order but a capitalist one. His case against the French principles was the same as his case against the Speenhamland principle: both would destroy traditional society by destroying the prerequisite condition of capitalist accumulation, that is, a submissive wage-earning class.

The argument that the wage relation is equitable is quite clear and can be put, as Burke did put it, either on utilitarian or on Natural Law grounds. The utilitarian argument runs: con-

tinuous capital accumulation is a prerequisite of civilisation;
accumulation (in any but a slave or servile society, which is
unacceptable) requires a wage-labour force whose wage leaves
a profit for the capital which employs it; that can be assured
if and only if the determination of wages is left to the impersonal market forces of supply and demand; those market
forces, being impersonal, are neither arbitrary nor based on
physical force, and are therefore equitable; therefore what must,
and may in good conscience, be upheld, is the capitalist order,
in spite of the hardship it sometimes inflicts on the labouring
poor.

On Natural Law grounds the argument is shorter but shak-
ier: what is divinely ordained must be equitable, the wage-
labour/capital relation is part of the divinely ordained natural
order, therefore it is equitable. The minor premise here, that the
capitalist order is part of the divine and natural order, is not
self-evident: indeed, at least until the end of the sixteenth century most writers and preachers would have treated it as non-
sense. But Burke needed the natural and divine law because he
had to show not only that the capitalist order was just but also
that it was naturally acceptable to the working class. The whole
structure of society, Burke insisted, depended on their sub-
missiveness. And he estimated that they would remain submissive if they were protected from the "rights of man"
principles by a counter-barrage of Christian Natural Law principles.

Burke was more astute than most of his contemporaries in
seeing that a revival of Christian Natural Law was just what
was needed. To make use of it, indeed, its content had to be
changed, for it had on the whole been sharply critical of market
morality. Its concept of justice, both distributive and commutative, had been based on customary norms and had been
used to defend the medieval and early modern society, a society
of custom and status, against the encroachments of the market.

Was Burke, then, doing violence to the old Natural Law in
turning it to the support of the capitalist market order? Was his
assumption that the capitalist order was the traditional order an

outrageous one? I think not. For capitalist behaviour and capitalist morality, which had been making inroads on the earlier society throughout the sixteenth century, had got the upper hand in England by the middle of the seventeenth. The property law and the political institutions needed for full capitalist development were well in place when they were confirmed by the Whig Revolution in 1689. So by Burke's time the capitalist order *had in fact been* the traditional order in England for a whole century. And it had become so by inserting itself inside an older hierarchical order without altering either the political forms – King, Lords and Commons remained – or the most fundamental class gradation, that between owners, enterprisers and labourers.

So there is nothing surprising or inconsistent in Burke's championing at the same time the traditional English hierarchical society and the capitalist market economy. He believed in both, and believed that the latter needed the former.

One question, however, may still be asked: granted that Burke could consistently speak for both capitalism and the traditional order *in England*, where they had already coalesced, what position could he consistently take about France and the rest of Europe, where they had not – where indeed capitalism had made little progress, any pressures for it being impeded by a political power structure compounded, in varying degrees in the continental realms and principalities, of feudalism and royal absolutism?

The question arises particularly in relation to Burke's attack on the French Revolution. Why should he have opposed it so vehemently, since in the view of most nineteenth-century historians, liberal as well as Marxist, it was essentially a bourgeois revolution, intent on clearing away feudal and absolutist impediments to the emergence of a capitalist order? If Burke's advocacy of tradition and inherited rights was, in the English context, at bottom an advocacy of a capitalist order, why should he not have applauded the revolution in France which, in assailing the inherited order there, was paving the way for a capitalist order on the Continent?

It is not a sufficient answer to say that, as we have already noticed, Burke's main concern was to check the spread of the French principles to England, for he was also concerned about Europe. He was, as he said near the beginning of the *Reflections*, 'sollicitous chiefly for the peace of my own country, but by no means unconcerned for your's'. He would, therefore,

set out with the proceedings of the [English] Revolution Society, but I shall not confine myself to them. Is it possible I should? It looks to me as if I were in a great crisis, not of the affairs of France alone, but of all Europe, perhaps of more than Europe. All circumstances taken together, the French revolution is the most astonishing that has hitherto happened in the world. (R 92)

Burke's realistic appraisal of the global importance of the revolution sharpens our question; why did he not at least moderate his assault on a revolution which, on the modern reading, would open the European states and their colonial dependencies to the beneficial operation of the capitalist market order?

The short answer is that Burke was not a nineteenth-century historian. He did not see modern history in terms of class conquests of power. Neither of the two revolutions of the seventeenth century in England appeared to him in that light, and it would be too much to expect that in 1790 he would see the French Revolution in the way that the nineteenth-century historians were to do. He did indeed scorn the type of men who, as the Third Estate, effectually controlled the French National Assembly, but he scorned them as pettyfogging local attorneys, quite unequipped to order the affairs of a nation. They were not the *haute bourgeoisie* who in England, easily intermarrying with the aristocracy, dominated the House of Commons: they were a *petite bourgeoisie*, who could not be relied on to uphold established property. The Assembly he found composed in large part of

obscure provincial advocates, of stewards of petty local jurisdictions, country attorneys, notaries, and the whole train of ministers of municipal litigation, the fomentors and conductors of the petty war of village vexation. (R 130)

And he predicted that it would end in the country being

wholly governed by the agitators in corporations, by societies in the towns formed of directors of assignats, and trustees for the sale of church lands, attornies, agents, money-jobbers, speculators, and adventurers ... (R 313)

What made such men unfit was not that they had no property, for they had a little and were greedy for more, but they had not the substantial settled property that gave the House of Commons its solidity. They had 'scarcely ... the slightest traces of what we call the natural landed interest of the country'; they were not distinguished as were the members of the House of Commons 'in rank, in descent, in hereditary and in acquired opulence, in cultivated talents, in military, civil, naval, and politic distinction ...' (R 132).

The only propertied men whom Burke saw as benefiting, at least in the short run, from the Revolution were the monied men whose wealth was in their holdings of the public debt. He noted that they had not merged, as monied men in England had done, with the nobility and the landed interest. In France 'the general circulation of property, and in particular the mutual convertibility of land into money, and of money into land, had always been a matter of difficulty'. Various provisions of French law 'had kept the landed and monied interests more separated in France, less miscible, and the owners of the two distinct species of property not so well disposed to each other as they are in this country' (R 209–10). These monied men, envious of the rank and titles from which they were shut out, were glad to strike at the nobility through the Crown and the Church, and to support the confiscation of Church lands. These 'money-jobbers' Burke scorned along with the 'obscure provincial advocates' and 'country attorneys', but he did not regard them as a class seeking a transformation of the economic order.

It is clear enough that Burke did not see the Revolution as a transfer of power to a substantial bourgeoisie, nor as removing feudal obstacles to a respectable bourgeois order that was waiting to emerge. Indeed he argued that, on the contrary, the Revolution might well be as damaging to commerce and industry as he expected it would be to the civilised arts and learning, since they had all grown to their present strength under the protection of the old regime:

commerce, and trade, and manufacture, the gods of our oeconomical politicians . . . certainly grew under the same shade in which learning flourished. They too may decay with their natural protecting principles. With you, for the present at least, they all threaten to disappear together. (R 174)

The transfer of power to the pettyfogging National Assembly he saw as a threat to, not an instrument of, capitalist advance in France. Besides, for all his historic bent, Burke believed as firmly as his very unhistorically minded contemporary, Bentham, that an attack on *any* established system of property was a threat to *every* kind of property. The innate rapacity of those with small or no property must run wild when any established system was breached. The present breach must be as devastating to emergent capitalism in France as it would be to established capitalism in England if the revolution were copied there. This was no mere abstract speculation, nor was it based only on history: it was already happening in France where the revolutionary government, moving on from their confiscation of the church lands,

have at length ventured completely to subvert all property of all descriptions throughout the extent of a great kingdom. They have compelled all men, in all transactions of commerce, in the disposal of lands, in civil dealing, and through the whole communion of life, to accept as perfect payment and good and lawful tender, the symbols of their speculations on a projected sale of their plunder. (R 261)

That Burke had some sense of a substantial bourgeois interest existing in France is suggested by the esteem in which he held Necker and Calonne, whose policies, in their short-lived terms of office as ministers of finance in the few years before 1789 might, if they had been accepted, have averted the Revolution. And we may assume that he was aware of the work of such French economists as Turgot, who had treated the capital/wage-labour relation as an obvious necessity, saying that 'every important enterprise of trade and industry requires the combination of two kinds of men, entrepreneurs and wage-workers ... This is the origin of the distinction between them, which is founded in the nature of things.'

Moreover, only on the assumption that Burke had some notion, however unclear, that there was in France a substantial bourgeois interest, is there any sense in his belief that the revolution in France could have been a mild Whig revolution. Yet that was his belief. The old French constitution, with its checks on royal power, could have been restored, as the English one had been in 1689.

Had you made it to be understood ... that you were resolved to resume your ancient privileges, whilst you preserved the spirit of your ancient and your recent loyalty and honour; or, if diffident of yourselves, and not clearly discerning the almost obliterated constitution of your ancestors, you had looked to your neighbours in this land, who had kept alive the ancient principles and models of the old common law of Europe meliorated and adapted to its present state – by following wise examples you would have given new examples of wisdom to the world. (R 123)

The French monarchy was not incapable of reform. The wealth and the population of the country had been steadily increasing, evidence enough that its government was not

so oppressive, or so corrupt, or so negligent, as to be utterly unfit *for all reformation.* I must think such a government well deserved to have its excellencies heightened; its faults corrected; and its capacities improved into a British constitution. (R 236)

Burke's notion that the French might in 1789 have brought off
something like the English Revolution of 1689 would be incred-
ibly naïve had he not been assuming some parallel in the forces
at work, a century apart, in the two countries. How far he saw
those forces in either case as specifically capitalist ones remains
doubtful. He did see clearly that England was a capitalist order,
but he did not put a date to the emergence of that order nor
attribute it to the Whig Revolution. The most we can say with
assurance is that he believed that France had been capable in
1789 of moving to something like the English Constitution, and
that the National Assembly had acted deliberately to *prevent*
that being done. He made that point explicitly in his first public
pronouncement on the Revolution, his *Speech on the Army
Estimates*, on 9 February 1790:

They brought themselves into all the calamities they suffer, not that
through them they might obtain a British constitution; they plunged
themselves headlong into those calamities, to prevent themselves
from settling into that constitution, or into anything resembling it.
(AE 5.14)

The French Revolution was just the reverse of the English one.
The English had changed kings but left the constitution un-
altered. 'Accordingly the state flourished ... An area of a more
improved domestic prosperity then commenced, and still con-
tinues ... All the energies of the country were awakened'
(AE 5.20–21).

Burke's denunciation of the French Revolution is thus not
only consistent with, but logically follows from, his praise of
the Whig Revolution. And since he linked the Whig Revolution
with the 'improved domestic prosperity' that had then commenced in England, and condemned the French Revolution as
having 'laid the axe to the root of all property, and consequently of all national prosperity' (AE 5.13), it is perhaps not
too much to see a bourgeois consistency in his treatment of the
two revolutions.

However, to return to Burke's overriding concern with the
situation in England, we have seen that he was not entirely

wrong in treating the capitalist society there as traditional society. It is true that the market was not yet absolutely triumphant in England. Humanitarian voices from within the establishment were still sometimes raised against it, as by the Speenhamland Justices. This made it all the more important for Burke to try to prevent such voices being pressed into common cause with the much more dangerous new French ideology.

His genius was in seeing that the capitalist society of the late eighteenth century was still heavily dependent on the acceptance of status. Contract had not replaced status: it was dependent on status. Burke's historical view was, for his time at least, more valid than the view of nineteenth-century analysts such as Sir Henry Maine, which is still apt to be taken as the received wisdom, namely, that the movement of the last few centuries had been a movement from status to contract. Burke saw that, down to his own time, such movement as there had been was not from status to contract but from status to status, that is, from a feudal status differentiation, which rested on military capacity, to what we should now call an internalised status differentiation, which rested on nothing more than habit and tradition, that is, on the subordinate class continuing to accept its traditional station in life. With no more solid basis than that, it could easily be undermined. Burke, recognising that fragility, had no recourse except to enlist Christian Natural Law in its aid. And this did no violence to the Christian Natural Law. It had always upheld a traditional social order against any threats. Now the content of the social order had changed, and in England it had changed long enough ago that the new content had already become traditional. So the Natural Law could now appropriately be used to defend the new traditional social order against new threats, the more so since the new content utilised the old forms.

Thus Burke is not to be condemned for twisting Christian Natural Law through a hundred and eighty degrees, but is to be commended for having seen that society had moved through the same arc. This, however, does not exonerate those who present Burke as a pure Christian Natural Law man without seeing that he had put a new bourgeois content into Natural Law. That misses Burke's real insight. And it begs the question of how useful a return to Burke would be in the late twentieth century.

6 Burke for the late twentieth century?

The Burke problem as set out in the opening pages of this study has perhaps now been sufficiently dealt with. We have seen that Burke was both a defender of a traditional hierarchical social and political order and a believer in the necessity and equity of a pure capitalist economic order. He could hold both positions consistently in so far as the capitalist economy had inserted itself inside the traditional social order and had changed the content though not the form of that order. That change had substantially taken place a century earlier, so that, in spite of such rearguard actions as Speenhamland, the new order was now the traditional one. How fully Burke saw the change is doubtful: he liked to link his traditional society back not only to 1689 but to Magna Carta, and to cover it all with the same Christian Natural Law. But what is not doubtful is his strong sense that the capitalist order could only be maintained if the working class continued to accept its traditional subordinate position. That sense lay behind his invocations of divine and natural law, and his carelessness or ignorance as to how much its content had changed. Utility and Natural Law were the same because capitalism and the traditional order were the same, because capitalism needed the sanction of tradition and habit. What put Burke ahead of many of his contemporaries was his perception that this was so.

But this view of Burke's insight in his own time raises a new question. How relevant is it to our time? What use can properly be made of him now by those who are seeking to retain or revive moral values in late twentieth-century Western societies in the face of the dangers by which they now seem to be beset? At first sight, not much use. For in spite of the persuasive efforts of a few economists such as Milton Friedman, it is no longer politically realistic for conservatives to try to take us back to a pure *laissez-faire* market economy; and liberal theorists who have accepted the modified capitalism of the welfare state do not seem to have much to gain from Burke's appeal to tradition.

Of course Burke's insistence on the rule of law, on constitutional versus arbitrary government, and on the respect due to property, is agreeable to both conservatives and liberals. And his case for letting a 'natural aristocracy' interpret and implement the real will of the people would be welcome enough to both; though they might not be willing to avow it, it is not too far from the idea of meritocracy to which they both subscribe in some measure. The real difficulty seems to lie in Burke's idea of distributive justice: the just distribution of the national product is that which the free market allots to those who enter the market from positions of class domination and subordination. That concept of justice cannot now be accepted or avowed by either conservatives or liberals; and it seems to be especially obnoxious to welfare-state liberals, since they start from the postulate of equal natural rights.

Nevertheless, the most renowned current liberal theory of distributive justice, namely John Rawls's *A Theory of Justice* (1971), is not fundamentally different from Burke's. Rawls accepts the welfare-state distribution up to a certain limit, but the limit is set on precisely the same principle as Burke's zero limit. Rawls holds that state interference with the market, intended to be in the interests of the poor, must stop short of the point at which it would make everybody, including the poor, worse off; and that that point is reached when the degree of interference would discourage enterprisers from continuing their work of maximising efficient production. This, as we have seen, was also Burke's position. The only difference is that Burke argued that *any* interference would have this effect, whereas the twentieth-century liberals have learned from experience that capitalist enterprise is still very active when it has to contend with the present quite substantial amount of state interference. The difference is not one of principle but of empirical judgement.

It appears, then, that if current liberals were to point this out they might well enlist Burke, the more readily in view of

Burke's lifelong insistence that circumstances alter cases and that statesmen and projectors should always devise their policies in the light of changing circumstances.

But the risks of enlisting Burke in this way would be considerable, for the change in circumstances between his time and ours is greater than we have noticed so far. The liberal task now is different from Burke's task. His was to persuade the English (and European) ruling class to resist any ideas which would weaken the still prevailing working-class acceptance of the established hierarchical order. He did not have to speak to the working class, nor did he do so. Now, however, the main liberal task is to legitimate the presently established modified capitalist order, or some variant of it, in the eyes of a somewhat politically conscious and quite strongly organised Western working class. And this has to be done in quite changed international circumstances.

No one was more aware than Burke that national policies needed to be framed in the light of the international situation. But when Burke died, in 1797, the egalitarianism of the French revolutionary theory and practice, while it was indeed a menace to the established English and European order, was still just a menace. Its outcome was still uncertain. It is so no longer. Now, the egalitarian principle is the official ideology of the communist world and the Third World, and their acceptance of it lies uneasily on the conscience of liberals in the Western world, who are not at all sure that the Western devotion to the egalitarian principle is more than skin-deep.

The twentieth-century liberals' problem is compounded in so far as they recognise that the utilitarian case for capitalism is no longer morally adequate. Moral theorists and political economists in the eighteenth century and well into the nineteenth could make a reasonable case for capitalism on the ground that a system of competitive enterprise moved by capital's search for profit would maximise production and hence conduce to maximum general benefit. But as capitalism has moved away from pure competition to oligopoly and monopoly it has become evident that capital's devotion to profit no longer necessarily maximises production or general benefit: in the new circumstances maximum profit is not tied to maximum productivity. To the extent that this is recognised, the potential usefulness of Burke's principles is further diminished. Not only must a case be made to a different national and international audience, it must be made without one of the main moral props of the old case.

To sum up: twentieth-century democrats, both liberal and conservative, share with Burke, the non-democrat, the perception that what is at stake is the legitimation of a social order, and that this is ultimately a question of moral values. They share, also, some of Burke's most general moral values. But if they heed Burke's warning about the vital necessity of adjusting principles to concrete circumstances, they must think twice about recruiting him. By his insistence on the importance of circumstances Burke ruled himself out of court for the late twentieth century.

Note on Sources

Citations of and quotations from works other than Burke's are as follows.

On p. 2, the two-volume study is Carl B. Cone, *Burke and the Nature of Politics* (University of Kentucky Press, 1957 and 1964). The four further studies in the 1950s and 60s are Charles Parkin, *The Moral Basis of Burke's Political Thought* (Cambridge University Press, 1956); Peter Stanlis, *Edmund Burke and the Natural Law* (University of Michigan Press, 1958); F. Canavan, *The Political Reason of Edmund Burke* (Durham, North Carolina, 1960); B. T. Wilkins, *The Problem of Burke's Political Philosophy* (Oxford, Clarendon Press, 1967). The more recent study is Frank O'Gorman, *Edmund Burke, his Political Philosophy* (London, Allen & Unwin, 1973). The psychobiography is Isaac Kramnick, *The Rage of Edmund Burke, Portrait of an Ambivalent Conservative* (New York, Basic Books, 1977).

On pp. 3–4, Gibbon's remark is from *The Private Letters of Edward Gibbon*, ed. R. E. Prothero (1897), vol. 2, p. 237; Marx's epithets are in *Capital*, vol. 1, ed. Dona Torr (London, Allen & Unwin, 1949), ch. 13, p. 312, and ch. 31, p. 785, n. 2. Morley's two books are *Edmund Burke, a Historical Study* (1867) and *Burke* (English Men of Letters) (1879). Buckle's remarks are in H. Buckle, *History of Civilization in England* (2nd ed., 1871), vol. 1, p. 467. Laski's view is in H. J. Laski, *Political Thought in England from Locke to Bentham* (London, Thornton Butterworth, 1920).

On p. 9, the reference to Kramnick is to his *The Rage of Edmund Burke*, pp. 59–63, where the flavour of this youthful Burke performance is displayed in several extracts from the *Reformer*.

On p. 11, details of Burke's involvement in the *Annual Register* are given in Cone, vol. 1, pp. 112–13 and 121–2.

On pp. 13–14, the first quotation from Morley is from his *Edmund Burke, a Historical Study*, p. 10; the second is from his article on Burke in the 11th ed. of the *Encyclopaedia Britannica.* The quotations from Laski are from H. J. Laski, *Political Thought in England from Locke to Bentham*, pp. 173–4.

On pp. 16–17, the quotation from Parkin is from his *The Moral Basis of Burke's Political Thought*, p. 3; those from Stanlis are from his *Edmund Burke and the Natural Law*, pp. 34, 4, and 83.

On pp. 21–2, the report of Adam Smith's remark is in Robert Bisset, *Life of Edmund Burke* (2nd ed., London, 1800), vol 2, p. 429.

On pp. 34–5 the quotations from Paine are from the *Rights of Man*, ed. H. B. Bonner, 1937, pp. 23, 29, 41; the quotation from Mackintosh is from *Vindiciae Gallicae*, 3rd ed., 1791, pp. vi–vii.

On pp. 35–6, the quotation from Morley is from *Edmund Burke, a Historical Study* (see above), pp. 25–6.

On p. 67, the quotation from Turgot is translated from *Oeuvres*, vol. 5, p. 244.

Further Reading

Writings by Burke

The *Reflections on the Revolution in France* is still fascinating reading, more for its pyrotechnics and the insight it gives the reader into Burke's thinking, than for its (faulty) analysis of the revolution. A recommended modern paperback edition is the one in Pelican Classics, with an introduction by Conor Cruise O'Brien. Equally important is Burke's much shorter *Thoughts and Details on Scarcity*, which is unfortunately not now in print but can be consulted in one or another edition of his works. Of his other writings the *Appeal from the New to the Old Whigs* is probably the most significant, but it is also not readily available. Readers interested in Burke the man may want to dip into the nine-volume *Correspondence* edited by T. W. Copeland, Cambridge University Press 1958–70.

Writings about Burke

The revival of interest in Burke in the last three decades has produced a variety of books and articles, as mentioned in Chapter I and the Note on Sources. Three of the books can be recommended, on different grounds. Carl B. Cone's *Burke and the Nature of Politics* (two volumes, 1957 and 1964, University of Kentucky Press) remains the most substantial modern study of Burke's life and work. A shorter work, Frank O'Gorman's *Edmund Burke, his Political Philosophy* (London, Allen and Unwin, 1973) gives an excellent conspectus of his political thought and corrects some of the claims that others (including Cone) had made. Still more recent is the enlivening though highly contentious psychobiography by Isaac Kramnick: *The Rage of Edmund Burke, Portrait of an Ambivalent Conservative* (New York, Basic Books, 1977).

Index

accumulation, desire for, see also avarice, 21, 44, 47, 53–4, 61–2

aesthetics, 10, 19

agriculture, 8–9, 52, 57, 59–60

America, 2–3, 13–14, 16–17, 26–7, 51

American War of Independence, 7, 15

aristocracy, see also landowners, 5–6, 8–9, 25, 39–40, 47, 64, 72

authority, see also liberty, political power, 14–15

avarice, see also accumulation, desire for, 21, 28, 54, 57

Bedford, Russell Francis, 5th Duke of, 5

Bentham, Jeremy, 18, 66

Bolingbroke, Henry, Viscount, 1, 10, 17–18

bourgeoisie, 63–7

Bristol (Burke's constituency), 5, 12, 25, 51

British Constitution – see Constitution (English)

Buckle, Henry Thomas, 4

BURKE, Edmund, family, 8–11; education, 8–10; legal career, 9–10; journalistic career, 11–12; literary career, 1, 9–11; political career, 11–37; economic theories, 3, 5, 18, 21–2, 51–70; as liberal, 3–4, 6, 12, 14; as conservative, 3, 12; as bourgeois, 3–4, 6, 9, 20–2, 25, 52, 68, 70; as pragmatist, 14–16, 19–20, 22–4, 26–7, 30, 36–7, 73–4; style and rhetoric, 34–7, 46; inconsistencies in arguments, 1–7; (ed) *Annual Register*, 11; *Appeal from the New to the Old Whigs*, 25, 39, 41, 44–8; *The Correspondence of Edmund Burke*, 2, 30; *An Essay Towards an Abridgement of the English History*, 11; *Letter to a Member of the National Assembly*, 43; *Letter to a Noble Lord*, 5–6, 30, 51; *Letter to Sir Hercules Langrishe*, 49; *Letter to the Sheriffs of Bristol on the Affairs of America*, 14, 27; *Letters on a Regicide Peace*, 5, 11, 21, 25, 48–9, 52–3, 55, 59; *Observations on a Late Publication Intituled the Present State of the Nation*, 22, 51; *A Philosophical Enquiry into the Origin of Our Ideas of the Sublime and Beautiful*, 10, 17, 19; *Reflections on the Revolution in France and on the Proceedings in Certain Societies in London Relative to that Event*, 1, 3, 5, 21, 34–5, 38–9, 41–3, 45, 47–9, 52, 54, 58, 60, 64–7; *Speech*

at the Close of the
Impeachment, 36; *Speech on
American Taxation*, 26;
Speech on Economical Reform,
5, 27–30, 52; *Speech on
Fox's East India Bill*, 31–3;
*Speech on Moving his
Resolutions for Conciliation
with the Colonies*, 26–7;
*Speech on Opening the
Articles of Impeachment*, 33–
4; *Speech on the Army
Estimates*, 68; *Speech on the
State of Representation of
the Commons in Parliament*,
40–1; *Thoughts and Details
on Scarcity*, 5, 21, 39, 52,
54–60; *Thoughts on the
Cause of the Present
Discontents*, 22–4, 28; *Tract
on the Popery Laws*, 19–21,
52, 54; *A Vindication of
Natural Society*, 10, 17–18,
51

Calonne, Charles Alexandre de,
67
capital, see also money, 42,
53–4, 56, 60–2, 67, 73
capitalism, see also market
economy, 5, 19, 53–4, 56,
58, 61–4, 66, 68–9, 71–3
Christianity, see also Church,
the, religion, 3
Christian Natural Law, see
also divine law, Natural Law,
49–50, 62, 69, 71
Church, The, see also
Christianity, religion, 6, 39,
65–6
Civil War, the (1642–49), 64
class relations, 9, 18, 48–9, 51,
63–4, 66, 69, 72; ruling
class, see also aristocracy,
landowners, 73; working

class, see also labourers,
58, 61–2, 71–2
'Club', the, 10, 21
colonies/colonial policies, see
America, India, Ireland
commerce, 3, 9, 30, 32, 51, 53,
57–9, 66
Commons, House of, see also
Lords, House of Parliament,
8, 12–13, 23, 26, 30, 33, 40,
63–5
communism, 4, 73
Comte, Auguste, 36
conservatism, 3, 7, 12–13, 16–
17, 71–2, 74
Constitution (English), 3, 12,
16, 22, 27, 38–41, 48–9,
67–8, 72
constitutional monarchy, see
also monarchy, 18, 68
contract, see also status, 33–4,
36, 45–7, 56, 59–60, 69
Court, the, see also Crown, the
monarchy, 2–3, 23–4
Crown, the, see also Court, the
monarchy, 23, 28–9, 39–40, 65

Declaration of Right, see also
rights, 39
demand, see also market
forces, supply, 56, 62
democracy, 4, 24, 74
divine law, see also Christian
Natural Law, Natural Law,
religion, 4, 31, 33–4, 36–7,
45, 53, 58–9, 62, 71
Dodsley, Robert, 11
Dublin, 8–9
duty, see also rights, 9, 11, 34,
38, 46, 58–9

East India Company, see also
India, 2–3, 30–3, 37, 51
economic affairs, 3, 5, 16, 18,
21–2, 37, 42, 51–70, 71

egalitarianism, see also equality, 3, 9, 39, 61, 72–3
eighteenth century, the, 1, 18, 46, 69, 73
empiricism, see also BURKE: as pragmatist, 19–21, 24, 26–9, 36, 72
employers, see also industry, landowners, production, 54, 56, 59–60
England, 5, 9, 17, 25, 37–9, 47, 51, 63–4, 66, 68–9
English Revolution Society, 7, 12, 17, 38–9, 61, 64
enterprise, see also *laissez-faire* policies, market economy, trade, 29, 52, 67, 72–3
enterpriser, 56, 63, 67, 72
equality, see also egalitarianism, 18, 20, 33–4, 43, 47, 72
equity, see also justice, 20, 29, 55, 58, 62, 71
Europe, see also France, French Revolution, 3, 11, 37–8, 51, 63–4, 73
expediency, see also BURKE: as pragmatist, empiricism, 13–14, 19, 23–4, 53, 73–4

Ferguson, Adam, 16
feudalism, 5, 28, 63, 66, 69
France, see also French Revolution, 4, 16, 38–9, 42, 44–5, 47, 49, 53, 63–4, 66–8
franchise, see also majority rule, representation, 22, 40, 48
French Revolution (1789), 3, 7, 12, 17, 33, 36–9, 42, 52, 61, 63–8, 73
Friedman, Milton, 71

Garrick, David, 10
George III, 3, 33

Gibbon, Edward, 3
Glorious Revolution (1689), see Whig Revolution
Goldsmith, Oliver, 10
government, 10, 13, 15, 22–7, 30, 38, 41, 44, 57–9, 67, 72

Hamilton, William Gerard, M.P., 11, 19
Hastings, Warren, 30–1, 33
Henry VIII, 5
hierarchical society, 3–4, 6–7, 44, 60–3, 69, 71, 73
history, 11, 24, 27, 30, 64, 66
Hobbes, Thomas, 20, 38, 42, 58
human nature, see also prejudice, reason, 20–2, 38, 42
Hume, David, 11, 16

India, see also East India Company, 3, 13, 16–17, 30–1, 36–7
industry, 21, 59, 66–7
inherited rights, 4–5, 39–40, 46, 63
Ireland, 3, 8–9, 11, 13, 16–17, 19–20, 51

Jacobins, 49
Johnson, Samuel, 10
justice, see also equity, 13, 17–18, 20, 43–4, 48, 57–8, 62, 72

Kramnick, Isaac, 9

labour, see also wages, 44, 53–6, 58, 61–2, 67
labourers, 52, 54–5, 57–60, 63, 67
laissez-faire policies, see also market economy, 29, 53, 71
land, 20, 65–6
landowners, see also aristocracy, 9, 24, 54, 64, 65

Laski, Harold, 4, 14
law, see also BURKE: legal
    career, 9–10, 15, 18, 20–1,
    25, 29, 31, 43–4, 72
liberalism, 3–4, 6–7, 12–14,
    16–17, 35, 63, 71–4
liberty, see also authority, 15,
    17, 27, 40–1
Locke, John, 3, 16, 32–4, 38, 42
London, 9–10, 12
Lords, House of, see also
    Commons, House of,
    Parliament, 33, 36, 63

Mackintosh, James, 35
Magna Carta, 32, 39, 71
Maine, Sir Henry, 69
majority rule, see also
    franchise, representation,
    46–7
manufacture, see production
market economy, see also
    capitalism, 3–4, 7, 29, 53,
    58, 62–4, 69, 71–2
market forces, see also
    demand, supply, 52, 55–7,
    59, 62
Marx, Karl, 3, 19
Marxism, 63
materialism, 16
meritocracy, 72
middle ages, 2, 62
Mill, John Stuart, 18
Millar, John, 16
monarchy, see also
    constitutional monarchy,
    Court, the, Crown, the, 18,
    23, 26, 63, 67
money, see also capital, rich,
    the, wealth, 54, 65–6
monopoly, 32, 73
morality, 13–14, 16, 18–19,
    24–5, 27, 29, 31, 41, 62–3,
    71, 73–4
Morley, John, 3, 13–14, 35–6

National Assembly (French),
    64–6, 68
Natural Law, 2, 4, 7, 16, 24,
    27, 32, 36, 61–2, 69–71;
    natural law (Burke's
    development of Natural
    Law), see also Christian
    Natural law, divine law, 37,
    49–50, 70–1
Necker, Jacques, 67
nineteenth century, the, 1, 3,
    12–13, 23, 35, 63–4, 69, 73

oligopoly, 73

Paine, Tom, 8, 17, 34–5
Parkin, Charles, 16
Parliament, see also Commons,
    House of, Lords, House of,
    1–2, 14, 17, 23, 25, 28, 30,
    33, 51
party and the two-party
    system, 6, 21–5
peasants, see also agriculture,
    labourers, 8, 53
'people, the' 24–6, 40, 44–5,
    61, 72
political economy, 5, 39, 50–
    70, 73
political institutions, 40, 63,
    71
political philosophy, 2, 16–19,
    35
political power, 22, 24, 29,
    32–3, 43, 63–6
political theory, 38, 42, 52
politics, 11, 13–14, 22
poor, the, see also labourers,
    rich, the, 18, 54–5, 57–8, 62
poor relief, see also state
    intervention, welfare state,
    52, 55, 59, 72
poverty, see also
    redistribution of wealth,
    wealth, 8–9, 55

positivism, 16, 36
prejudice, see also human nature, reason, 4, 25, 35, 41–2
prescriptive rights, 4–5, 41, 46
Price, Richard, 17
Priestley, Joseph, 17
production, see also industry, 53–4, 56, 66, 72–4
profit, 28, 53–6, 62, 73–4
property rights, 5, 9, 20–1, 24, 30, 32, 37, 39, 41, 47, 52, 57, 59, 61, 63–6, 68, 72
prosperity, see also rich, the, wealth, 21, 53–4, 59, 68

radicalism, 4
rationalists, 3, 46
Rawls, John, 72
reason, see also human nature, prejudice, 4, 22, 27, 41–2
redistribution of wealth, see also wealth, 47, 55
reform, 2, 5, 9, 13, 22, 27–30, 40–1, 67
religion, see also Christianity, Christian Natural Law, Church, the, divine law, 8, 10, 17–18, 20, 44, 61
religious toleration, 3
representation, see also franchise, majority rule, 25, 46–9
revolution, see English Revolution Society, French Revolution, Whig Revolution
Reynolds, Sir Joshua, 10
rich, the, see also money, poor, the, prosperity, 8, 18, 37, 47, 54–5, 59, 65
rights, see also Declaration of Right, duties, 15, 20, 26–7, 31–4, 39–40, 42–4, 46
'rights of man', 33, 43–5, 62

Rockingham, Marquis of, 6, 12, 19, 22–3, 26
Rousseau, Jean-Jacques, 10, 18–19

seventeenth century, the, 26–7, 63–4
Sheridan, Richard, 10
sixteenth century, the, 62–3
Smith, Adam, 10, 21, 53, 59
social contract, see contract
society, 5, 10, 18, 20, 38, 42–6, 50, 52, 58, 62, 69, 73–4
Speenhamland, 52, 61, 69, 71
Stanlis, Peter, 16
state, the, 5, 21, 43–8, 53–4, 68
state intervention, see also poor relief, welfare state, 56–9, 72
status, see also contract, 8, 59, 62, 69
supply, see also demand, market forces, 56, 62

taxation, 26, 52
Third Estate (France), 64
Third World, 73
trade, see also market economy, 29–30, 56, 66–7
traditionalism, 4, 6, 28
traditional society, 3, 5, 61–3, 69, 71–2
Turgot, Anne Robert Jacques, 67
twentieth century, the, 1, 4, 7, 12–13, 16, 36, 46, 70–4

utilitarianism, 3–4, 7, 16, 21, 30, 40, 47, 61–2, 73
utility, 20–1, 27, 40, 60 71

Verney, Lord, 12

wages/the wage relation, 55–62

wage labour, *see* labour
wealth, *see also* prosperity,
  redistribution of wealth,
  5–6, 9, 21, 28, 54, 65
welfare state, *see also* poor
  relief, state intervention,
  72

Wendover (Burke's
  constituency), 12
Whigs, 2, 6, 12–13, 19, 23,
  32–4
Whig Revolution (1689), 3, 7,
  16, 39, 63–4, 67–8, 71
Wilkes case, the (1763), 17

Past Masters

MARX Peter Singer

Peter Singer identifies the central vision that unifies Marx's thought, enabling us to grasp Marx's views as a whole. He views him as a philosopher primarily concerned with human freedom, rather than as an economist or social scientist. He explains alienation, historical materialism, the economic theory of *Capital*, and Marx's idea of communism, in plain English, and concludes with a balanced assessment of Marx's achievement.

PASCAL Alban Krailsheimer

Alban Krailsheimer opens his study of Pascal's life and work with a description of Pascal's religious conversion, and then discusses his literary, mathematical and scientific achievements, which culminated in the acute analysis of human character and powerful reasoning of the *Pensées*. He argues that after his conversion Pascal put his previous work in a different perspective and saw his, and in general all human activity, in religious terms.

Past Masters

AQUINAS Anthony Kenny

Anthony Kenny writes about Thomas Aquinas as a philosopher, for readers who may not share Aquinas's theological interests and beliefs. He begins with an account of Aquinas's life and works, and assesses his importance for contemporary philosophy. The book is completed by more detailed examinations of Aquinas's metaphysical system and his philosophy of mind.

DANTE George Holmes

George Holmes expresses Dante's powerful originality by identifying the unexpected connections the poet made between received ideas and his own experience. He presents Dante's biography both as an expression of the intellectual dilemma of early Renaissance Florence and as an explanation of the poetic, philosophical and religious themes developed in his works. He ends with a discussion of the *Divine Comedy*, Dante's poetic panorama of hell, purgatory and heaven.

JESUS Humphrey Carpenter

Humphrey Carpenter writes about Jesus from the standpoint of a historian coming fresh to the subject without religious preconceptions. He examines the reliability of the Gospels, the originality of Jesus's teaching, and Jesus's view of himself. His highly readable book achieves a remarkable degree of objectivity about a subject which is deeply embedded in Western culture.

K. J. Dover and others

ANCIENT GREEK LITERATURE

K. J. Dover and three other classical scholars have collaborated in writing this new historical survey of Greek literature from 700 BC to AD 550. The book concentrates on the principal authors and quotes many passages from their work in translation, to allow the reader to form his own impression of its quality. Attention is drawn both to the elements in Greek literature and attitudes to life which are unfamiliar to us, and to the elements which appeal most powerfully to succeeding generations. Although it is recognized that this appeal lies above all in the most creative and inventive period (700–300 BC), an account is given of the eight hundred years which followed, which saw the results of earlier inspirations. Poetry, tragedy, comedy, history, science, philosophy, and oratory are all examined through the available literature.

Homer

THE ODYSSEY

A new translation by Walter Shewring

By its evocation of an heroic age, its contrasts of character and variety of adventure, above all by its sheer narrative power, *The Odyssey* has won and preserved its place among the greatest tales in the world. It recounts Odysseus' wanderings as he returns from the long war at Troy – the hazards he encounters, his visit to the underworld, and his arrival home, where he plots revenge on the insolent suitors who have for years besieged his wife, Penelope.

It is hard in any modern version of Homer to reconcile the easy flow of the story-telling with the poet's formal uncolloquial style. Walter Shewring's new attempt does this so successfully that it will surely be regarded as one of the few really outstanding translations of *The Odyssey*.